VOLCANO

VOLCANO

LIVE, DORMANT AND EXTINCT VOLCANOES AROUND THE WORLD

ROBERT J. FORD

amber
BOOKS

This Amber edition first published in 2023

First published in a landscape format edition in 2021

Published by Amber Books Ltd
United House
North Road
London
N7 9DP
United Kingdom
www.amberbooks.co.uk
Instagram: amberbooksltd
Facebook: amberbooks
Twitter: @amberbooks
Pinterest: amberbooksltd

ISBN: 978-1-83886-311-1

Project Editor: Anna Brownbridge
Designer: Keren Harragan
Picture Research: Terry Forshaw

Printed in China

Contents

Introduction

We humans have felt for centuries that we have mastery over our world – transforming it to suit our needs and ways of life.

Yet our planet now and again sends reminders that we are but residents upon its back. Volcanoes are the most powerful of these, which humans snuggled up against over time as we expand our built environment into every corner of the natural world. Some appear harmless – simply extinct mountains that dominate the skyscape – although they serve as stark lessons on the earth's tumultuous past to those who are paying attention; others cannot be ignored, as the full force of the planet's interior is violently thrust upon the earth's surface in the form of lava explosions, lava bombs, pyroclastic flows and ash clouds that blanket the sky and shut out the day.

This book is a visual examination of the world's most impressive, infamous and most active volcanoes from all corners of the globe. From mountains towering over conurbations to remote and unobtrusive yet fiery fissures in the crust, and from ancient sleeping giants to volcanoes born in the last century – as well as, of course, the most stunning, extreme eruptions – this is a look at the sheer power and majesty our planet still holds, and of which we should all be wary.

OPPOSITE:
Kilauea, Hawaii, Hawaiian Islands
Kilauea is the most active of the five volcanoes that form the island.

Europe

EUROPEANS are among the world's oldest volcanologists. The earliest known documentation of volcanism is an Anatolian wall painting of a nearby cinder cone eruption around 6200 BC; the vigorous historic record of Etna in Sicily goes back to 1500 BC; and the catastrophic eruption of Vesuvius in AD 79, with the burial of Pompeii, continues to serve today as an object lesson in the perils of living near a volcano.

The region has given us the first documented 'new' mountain, Monte Nuovo, in 1538, the first 'new island' at Santorini, in 197 BC, and the word 'volcano' itself comes from the Latin 'Vulcan' – the Roman god of fire. Europe may lack the volcanic magnificence of Indonesia, the grandeur of the Andes, the destructiveness of a St Helens or the beauty of a Fuji, yet there are currently more than 60 active volcanoes located in Europe, the best known being Mount Etna in Sicily and Mount Vesuvius on the Italian mainland. The Icelandic volcano Eyjafjallajökull made news headlines for weeks after a 2010 explosion.

European volcanoes and their eruptions also lend their names to several types of volcanic eruption, such as Strombolian, Plinian and Vulcanian. So while Europe may not be as big a player in terms of volcanism as other continents these days, it has nevertheless indelibly marked its past on the canvas of global historical volcanic activity.

OPPOSITE:
Kirkjufell, Snæfellsnes peninsula, Iceland
Jutting into the sea on Snæfellsnes peninsula, this 463m (1519ft) high mountain is the most photographed in Iceland. Consisting of layers deposited from numerous volcanic eruptions and glacial periods, its exposed peak once sat between two ancient glaciers, which ground down the mountain's sides to leave the steeple-like summit that gives 'Church Mountain' its name. It has attracted recent attention for its appearance as the 'arrowhead mountain' in iconic scenes north of the Wall in *Game of Thrones* Seasons 6 and 7.

ABOVE:
Holuhraun lava field, Suður-Þingeyjarsýsla, Iceland
In late August 2014, volcanic activity from the Bárðarbunga volcanic system caused a large fissure to open up in the Holuhraun lava field, which, over the course of six months, spewed out around 1.6 cubic km (0.38 cu mile) of lava, covering 85 square km (33 sq miles).

RIGHT:
Bárðarbunga volcanic system, Vatnajökull National Park, Iceland
Bárðarbunga is a stratovolcano located under the Vatnajökull ice cap (known as a subglacial volcano), Iceland's biggest. During the 2014–15 eruption, the emptying of Bárðarbunga's magma chamber saw a subsidence of its caldera by around 65m (213ft), which also caused a sinking of the surface of the glacier under which the volcano sits.

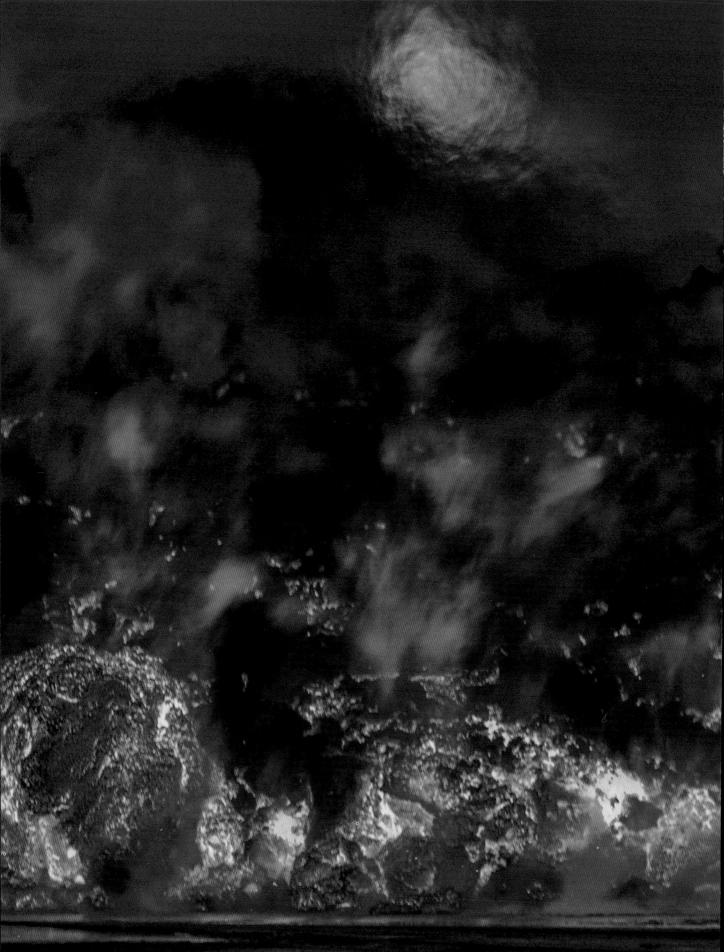

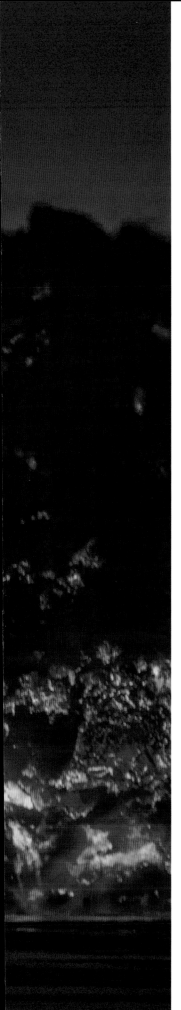

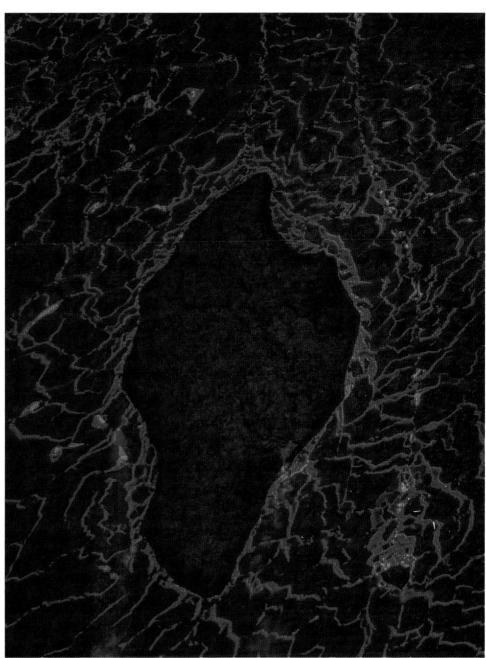

LEFT:

**Holuhraun lava field,
Suður-Þingeyjarsýsla, Iceland**

Glowing lava and smoke plumes mark the Holuhraun fissure in the hellish landscape of the 2014–15 eruption of the Bárðarbunga volcanic system. The six-month episode saw 9.6 million tonnes (9.4 million tons) of sulphur dioxide (SO_2) emitted into the atmosphere, 16 times more SO_2 than that produced in a year by humans in Iceland.

ABOVE:

**Holuhraun lava field,
Suður-Þingeyjarsýsla, Iceland**

The volcanic activity of 2014–15 was the biggest eruption in Iceland for more than 200 years, since the 1783–84 Laki eruption. This incident killed 50 per cent of livestock, 80 per cent of crops and 25 per cent of the human population in Iceland because of the eruption's poisonous gases, and is thought to have affected global temperatures.

Eldfell, Heimaey, Westman Islands, Iceland
Eldfell (right) is a very young volcano and is one of Iceland's most famous. It formed during a violent and unexpected eruption in 1973 that saw the entire island's population evacuated after a fissure opened up along the east side of the island, running from coast to coast, only 1km (0.6 miles) from the centre of town. Within two days a cinder cone 100m (330ft) high had been created, which doubled in height over the next few weeks to roughly its current standing. Huge lava flows threatened to cut off the harbour, one of the key locations for Iceland's fishing industry. By pumping seawater onto the advacing lava, the harbour was saved. Hundreds of houses, however, were buried by ash or destroyed by lava.

Eyjafjallajökull, Iceland
Eyjafjallajökull is a subglacial volcano – one made by activity beneath ice – that erupted in truly dramatic fashion in April and May 2010. Around 250 million cubic metres (8.8 billion cu ft) of tephra – the volcanic fragments produced during an eruption – was pumped into the air, creating a plume of ash, smoke and steam from the melting of the mountain's ice-filled crater that at times rose to a height of up to 9km (5.6 miles).

Eyjafjallajökull, Iceland
While not one of the most
powerful volcanic episodes,
it was the spread of ash, fine
particles and steam from the
volcano's glacial meltwater over
large parts of Europe that made
headlines during the eruption of
Eyjafjallajökull in 2010, with
its threat to the functioning of
aircraft engines resulting in the
biggest shutdown of air traffic
since World War II. In a period
of around a week in April,
100,000 flights were cancelled,
affecting about 10 million
people.

Eyjafjallajökull, Iceland
Iceland sits on the Mid-
Atlantic Ridge, the underwater
boundary between the Eurasian
and North American tectonic
plates. As these two plates
move apart, magma constantly
wells up along the ridge and
cools, creating new sea floor.
Beneath Iceland is a pocket
of particularly hot magma
that rose to the surface of the
ocean where it cooled and
accumulated to form the island
of Iceland. Because of Iceland's
position on this volcanically
unstable rift line, it is home to
numerous volcanoes and sees
regular geothermal and seismic
activity.

Eyjafjallajökull, Iceland
The 2010 eruption of
Eyjafjallajökull created
ideal conditions for the rare
phenomenon of volcanic
lightning. The collision of
material ejected from the
volcano's craters caused a
build-up of static electricity
in the atmosphere, which
when combined with the
accumulation of charge from
rising hot air and moisture from
the crater's meltwater reaching
many kilometres up, created a
huge amount of electricity that
needed to be discharged, leading
to spectacular, if hellish, sights.

**La Bourboule, Puy de Dôme,
Auvergne-Rhône-Alpes, France**
The town of La Bourboule, situated in a glacial valley at an altitude
of 852m (2795ft), is famous for its thermal waters, which are
enriched by the volcanic geology of the subsoil.
This is a remnant of the volcanic activity of members of France's
Massif Central mountain chain, situated near the middle of the
country, in which the town sits (pictured).

RIGHT TOP:

Chaîne des Puys, Auvergne-Rhône-Alpes, France

The Chaîne des Puys is a string of volcanoes 40km (25 miles) long, and part of France's Massif Central. Here the peak of Puy de Dôme can be seen from the crater of Puy de Pariou. The creation of the Alps fractured the crust in this region, allowing occasional wells of magma to rise up, with one episode forming the Chaîne des Puys from about 70,000 to about 11,700 years ago. These volcanoes have been dormant now for 6000 years.

RIGHT BOTTOM:

Puy de Pariou, Chaîne des Puys, Auvergne-Rhône-Alpes, France

About 1.5km (0.93 miles) north of Puy de Dôme is the Puy de Pariou. It is formed by two typically Strombolian cones, one crater sitting inside the other, a feature known as a somma volcano. The central crater is the younger and higher of the two at 1209m (3967ft). Only a part of the older cone remains, the rest being covered by a tuff ring.

OPPOSITE TOP:

Puy de Dôme, Chaîne des Puys, Auvergne-Rhône-Alpes, France

Puy de Dôme is the highest point of the Chaîne des Puys at 1465m (4806ft). Pictured is the north face of the volcano's lava dome, which was created by the expulsion of thick lava in a Peléan eruption around 10,700 years ago. Traits of Peléan eruptions are lava domes and violent avalanches of hot gas and volcanic matter known as pyroclastic flows.

Piton de la Fournaise, Réunion Island, Indian Ocean
This shield volcano on Réunion Island, a French *département*, is one of the most active volcanoes in the world. Its name translates as 'peak of the furnace', an indicator of how often it erupts, the most recent instance being in October 2019. Despite this, it is a popular tourist site, with visitors able to access the peak. A shield volcano is one with a low, broad profile with shallowly sloping sides that has been built up over time by repeated emissions of relatively fluid lava (usually basaltic). Shield volcanoes are characterized by their low explosivity and lack of pyroclastic material.

**Teide, Tenerife,
Canary Islands, Spain**
The highest point in Spain and
the islands of the Atlantic at
3718m (12,198ft), Teide rises
out of the caldera of another
giant volcano that helped birth
Tenerife. The island was created
through the accretions of three
large shield volcanoes that
formed their own small land
masses. Between these another
volcano, Las Cañadas, formed,
joining all four together in a
small island, which then grew
over the millennia. Las Cañadas
later collapsed to create the
caldera, out of which Teide
grew over the course of the last
160,000 years.

RIGHT TOP:

La Tarta outcrop, Teide National Park, Tenerife, Canary Islands, Spain

This outcrop of rock has preserved various episodes of Tenerife's volcanic activity by capturing the material ejected during eruptions at different times in the island's history. The white layers are made of pumice stone, the black layers are basaltic lava rocks, characteristic of eruptions with low gas emissions, and the reddish layers are basaltic materials that have oxidized after coming into contact with groundwater.

RIGHT MIDDLE:

Croscat, Garrotxa, Catalonia, Spain

The youngest and highest volcano on the Iberian peninsula, Croscat's cone has a horseshoe shape, its western side having collapsed, probably under consistent lava flow. The northeastern side (pictured) has been quarried away for gravel and provides a glimpse inside the volcano.

RIGHT BOTTOM:

Tahiche, Lanzarote, Canary Islands, Spain

This house sits on the remains of lava that cooled and solidified to create these unusual sculpted rock formations.

OPPOSITE

Calderón Hondo, Fuerteventura, Canary Islands, Spain

One of a series of volcanoes born around 50,000 years ago, Calderón Hondo – the crater of which reaches 278m (912ft) at its highest point – and its neighbours form the Bayuyo alignment, a 5km (3.1 miles) straight chain of volcanoes. Their lava expanded the territory of the island of Fuerteventura north into the sea and toward Lanzarote. This volcanism also helped birth the island of Lobos.

Timanfaya National Park, Lanzarote, Canary Islands, Spain
The beautiful volcanic landscape of Timanfaya was created over a six-year period of near-continuous volcanic activity between 1730 and 1736, with another, smaller episode in 1824. Vast quantities of lava spewed out from dozens of volcanoes onto previously fertile land during the eruptions, destroying a number of villages while expanding the land into the sea.

Timanfaya National Park was created over

ABOVE TOP:
Timanfaya National Park,
Lanzarote, Canary Islands, Spain
While there is still volcanic heating under the ground, creating temperatures a few metres below the surface of up to 600°C (1112°F), only one volcano – Timanfaya itself – remains active. The delicate ecosystem created by the historic volcanic activity has meant the park is carefully protected and tourism there strictly regulated.

ABOVE BOTTOM:
Mount Pico, Pico Island,
Azores, Portugal
This stratovolcano – a tall, conical-shaped volcano comprised of strata (layers) of lava, tephra, ash and pumice – has historically erupted from vents on its sides rather than at its summit crater because magma can travel through any of a stratovolcano's many underground passages. Stratovolcanoes are also known as composite volcanoes and are made of half lava and half pyroclastic material. They are the most explosive type of volcano.

RIGHT:
Islet of Vila Franca do Campo,
São Miguel Island, Azores,
Portugal
Situated opposite the town of Vila Franca do Campo on the island of São Miguel stands an islet formed by the crater of an ancient submerged volcano. Its walls are lined with vegetation endemic to the islet, while inside there is an almost perfectly circular natural lagoon. A small channel allows for the passage of water between the ocean and lagoon, allowing a rich marine life of crustaceans, fish and algae to blossom there.

Lagoa de Santiago, Sete Citades, São Miguel Island, Azores, Portugal

The Lagoa de Santiago fills one of the cones that arose in the caldera of the Sete Citades Massif, an ancient stratovolcanic complex at the western end of São Miguel Island. The caldera is dominated by the twin lake of Lagoa das Sete Citades (seen in the background), which is said to have been created by the tears of two young lovers forbidden to see each other by the king.

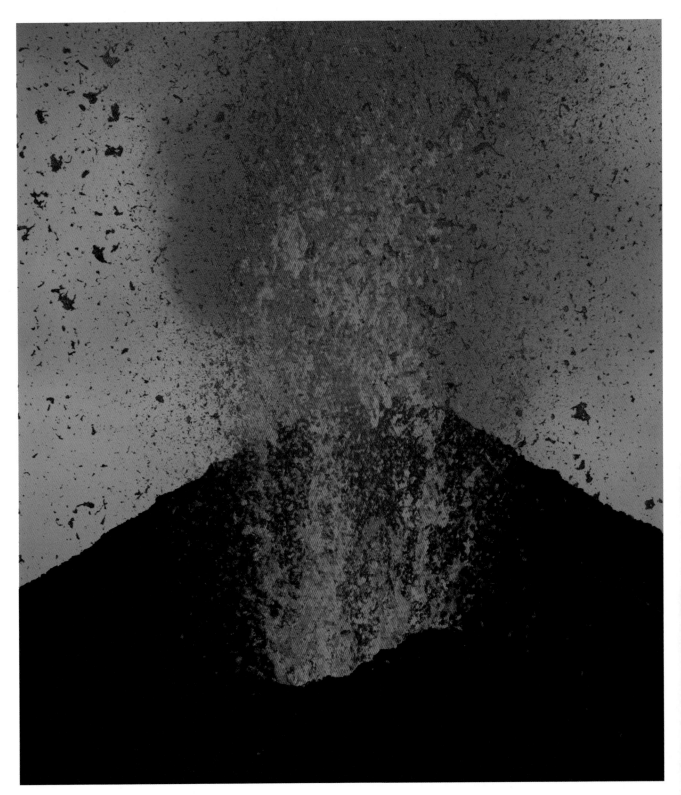

ABOVE:

Stromboli, Aeolian Islands, Italy

Active for at least 2000 years, and in mostly continual eruption since 1932, volcanic activity at Stromboli is usually mild, with brief yet spectacular explosions of glowing lava fragments up to 100–200m (328–656ft) high, with some ash and occasional lava flows. These episodes are so distinctive that geologists term similar examples at other volcanoes 'Strombolian'.

OPPOSITE:

Vulcano and Lipari, Aeolian Islands, Italy

'Vulcanian' eruptions – named after the island and volcano of Vulcan – are small, noisy, violent explosions of a dense cloud of ash-laden gas and rock, with both pyroclastic and thick magma flows. The Aeolians are part of a volcanic arc, including Lipari (centre), that formed from the subduction of the African tectonic plate under that of the Eurasian plate.

Mount Etna, Sicily, Italy
One of the few active volcanoes in Italy, Mount Etna's past eruptions are evidenced by the numerous craters and vents on the mountain's flanks (pictured). The International Association of Volcanology and Chemistry of the Earth's Interior has designated Etna a 'Decade Volcano', one of 16 volcanoes from around the world that have been deemed worthy of particularly close study because of their histories of destructive eruptions and locations near populated areas. The project promotes public awareness of these recently active volcanoes in order to reduce the impact of their eruptions. Other examples include Teide, Santorini and Vesuvius.

ABOVE:

Mount Etna, Sicily, Italy

Mount Etna is one of the world's most active volcanoes, due to its position over the converging African and Eurasian tectonic plates, which gives it a constant supply of volcanic material and gases. Here lava fountains up from one of five summit craters. Etna has had a number of flank and summit eruptions in the twenty-first century alone.

RIGHT:

Mazzarò, Sicily, Italy

A smoking Mount Etna looms over the ruins of Teatro Antico di Taormina, an ancient Greek theatre. The mountain consists of two volcanoes: a shield volcano that began erupting here about 500,000 years ago sits under a 35,000-year-old stratovolcano. Etna experiences a variety of eruption styles, including violent Strombolian explosions and frequent lava flows.

Mount Vesuvius, Campania, Italy
Mount Vesuvius, part of the Campanian Volcanic Arc, dominates the Bay of Naples and the population centres lying within its reach. It is these nearby settlements that make Vesuvius one of the most dangerous volcanoes in the world, with three million people in Naples near enough to be threatened by an eruption and the mountain being the only mainland European volcano to have erupted in the past 100 years (1944 being the last incident).

PREVIOUS PAGE:

AD 79 eruption of Mount Vesuvius, Pompeii, Campania, Italy

There have been many eruptions from Vesuvius since AD 79, but none have been as destructive as the one of that year. It threw a huge cloud of ash, stones and gases 15–30km (9–19 miles) high, ejected streams of molten rock and pumice, and most famously destroyed the cities of Pompeii and Herculaneum with pyroclastic surges, burying both settlements under many metres of tephra. Impressions of bodies overtaken by the ash tell just some of the horror of the story.

LEFT:

Mount Vesuvius, Campania, Italy

Vesuvius is what is known as a somma-stratovolcano – that is, a stratovolcano that sits inside the collapsed caldera of another, older volcano. The walls of the collapsed caldera can be seen here behind the central cone. The mountain lends its name to Vesuvian-type eruptions: those characterized by the ejection of columns of hot gases and ash into the stratosphere. The pyroclastic surges of AD 79, however, are typical of Peléan eruptions.

Nisyros, Dodecanese, Greece
Nisyros emerged from the sea around 150,000 years ago in three eruptive stages. The only eruptions in the last few thousand years, however, have been hydrothermal – where magma under the earth's surface heats groundwater or intrusive seawater to produce eruptions of steam, gas and rock, alongside earthquakes.

Stefanos crater, Nisyros, Dodecanese, Greece
Nisyros is a volcanic Greek island in the Aegean Sea. The volcano is still active, as indicated by fumaroles – openings that emit steam and gases – at some of the island's 20 craters. The largest and most imposing crater is 4000–5000-year-old Stefanos (pictured), 330m (1083ft) across at its widest point.

Nea Kameni, Santorini, Greece
Some 3600 years ago, several large, explosive volcanic eruptions formed the present island of Santorini, an origin now indicated clearly by the outline of the submerged caldera. More recent activity within the caldera birthed Nea Kameni (top right) 2000 years ago. These islands form part of the South Aegean Volcanic Arc, which marks the subduction of the African tectonic plate under the Aegean sub-plate of the Eurasian plate.

Mount Ararat, Turkey
Mount Ararat, near the
Turkey–Armenia border,
consists of two volcanoes:
Great Ararat and Little Ararat.
Great Ararat is the highest peak
in Turkey with an elevation of
5137m (16,854ft). Ararat is a
complex or compound volcano,
one that has changed either its
eruptive habit or location of the
main vent area. The mountain
is considered by some to be the
resting place of Noah's Ark.

Africa & the Middle East

FRICA has many dozens of active volcanoes, many of which are located along the East African Rift – a fault line that runs from Eritrea and Djibouti down to the Democratic Republic of Congo and Tanzania. The rift is caused by the breaking in two of the African continent; at the same time, it is moving away from the Arabian tectonic plate at a speed slower than the growth rate of a human fingernail. Spreading processes at the 'triple junction' these three plates meet at has already torn Saudi Arabia away from the rest of Africa to create new sea floor – what we know as the Red Sea and the Gulf of Aden, where the boundary between the African and Arabian plates lies. As the land has stretched, it has cracked and allowed molten rock to rise to the surface to erupt and form the volcanoes of the East African Rift. The rift has produced the continent's highest and lowest volcanoes – from the massive Kilimanjaro to vents in Ethiopia's Danakil Depression that lie below sea level.

While the Middle East may not boast the range and drama of some of the volcanoes in Africa, it nevertheless has its own unique area of volcanism. This is due to the collision between the Eurasian and Arabian plates, with eruptive activity focusing on Iran, including such magnificent, historical mountains as Damavand.

OPPOSITE:
Pico do Fogo, Fogo, Cape Verde
Pico do Fogo is the highest peak on the islands that make up Cape Verde, as well as in West Africa, standing at 2829m (9281ft). It is a stratovolcano with a summit caldera that last erupted in 1680, when much of the population left the island. A few other eruptions have occurred on the flanks since, including in 1995 when ash covered the island and lava fountains and lava bombs spewed forth, destroying a number of homes near the summit. Another magmatic eruption occurred in 2014–15.

LEFT:

**2014–15 eruption of Pico
do Fogo, Fogo, Cape Verde**
The 2014–15 Strombolian
eruption of Pico do Fogo ended
after 77 days of activity. Lava
flows travelled down some
roads and covered 4 square km
(1.5 sq miles), leaving strange
formations where it cooled. This
eruption surpassed that of the
1995 eruption in strength, and
approached that of the 1951
eruption, one of the strongest
ever recorded on the island.

ABOVE:

**2014–15 eruption of Pico
do Fogo, Fogo, Cape Verde**
The eruption stopped after
destroying 75 per cent of the
buildings in the villages of
Portela (pictured), Bangaeira
and Ilhéu de Losna, which
are located in the crater of the
volcano, by covering them in
lava.

**Mount Cameroon,
Buea, Cameroon**
Also known as Fako after the
higher of its two peaks, Mount
Cameroon has the fourth
highest summit in Africa at
4040m (13,255ft). It is part of
a 1600km (990 miles) chain
of mountains known as the
Cameroon line stretching from
the Gulf of Guinea northeast
into the African continent. It
has erupted seven times in the
last century and has more than
100 cones dotted over
its flanks and summit region.

Mount Cameroon, Buea, Cameroon
These craters mark the volcano's last eruption in 2000, which occurred at two sites on the mountain. The higher vents saw more explosive activity whereas the lower vents were the location of lava flows. These travelled across a nearby highway, and damaged forest and palm plantations in the village of Bakingili on the volcano's foothills, which led to the evacuation of its 600 inhabitants.

Mount Nyiragongo, Virunga National Park, Democratic Republic of the Congo
The main crater of the stratovolcano Nyiragongo is 2km (1.24 miles) wide and usually holds a lava lake – a volume of lava contained in a crater, vent or depression – part of which can be seen here still uncovered and active, emitting steam and gas. While the lake was once more voluminous, it is now mostly contained in a cinder cone on the crater floor.

Mount Nyiragongo, Virunga National Park, Democratic Republic of the Congo (DRC) This view of Mount Nyiragongo is from over Lake Kivu in Rwanda, the volcano being located close to the border between the DRC and Rwanda. It is part of a chain of eight volcanoes called the Virunga Mountains, part of the Albertine Rift Mountains on the western branch of the East African Rift. These mountains are the result of the rift made from the African tectonic plate splitting in two to become the Somali and Nubian plates.

LEFT:

Mount Nyiragongo, Virunga National Park, Democratic Republic of the Congo
Nyiragongo's lava lake has on occasion contained the greatest known volume of lava in such a lake, although it is thought to be much shallower than before a 1977 eruption, which drained it. Terraces within the crater indicate the level of old lava lakes. The volcano's lava is also unusually fluid and has been measured flowing down the mountain's steep slopes at speeds of almost 100km/h (60mph).

ABOVE:

Mount Nyiragongo, Virunga National Park, Democratic Republic of the Congo
Nowhere else does such a steep-sided stratovolcano contain a lake of such fluid lava. Because of its location near population centres, and the frequency of its eruptions, the chances of it causing widespread devastation are high. As such, it has been designated one of 16 Decade Volcanoes, the most dangerous in the world. In 2002 an eruption destroyed large swathes of the nearby city of Goma's commercial centre, prompting up to 200,000 to flee their homes.

Mount Kilimanjaro, Tanzania
Kilimanjaro is a dormant stratovolcano and the highest freestanding mountain in the world, and comprises three volcanic cones. The tallest, Kibo (right) is 5899m (19,354ft), while Mawenzi, at 5149m (16,893ft), can be seen to the left. Kibo has for millennia been covered by an ice cap that can still be seen. In the last century, however, it has retreated by 85 per cent and is expected to have mostly disappeared by 2040.

LEFT:

Ol Doinyo Lengai, Tanzania
The rim of arguably the most unusual volcano in the world. Ol Doinyo Lengai's impressive crater is currently the only place on earth that can erupt natrocarbonatite lava, which is crammed full of calcium, sodium, carbon dioxide and potassium, rather than the silicates in regular lava composition that give it its strength and viscosity.

ABOVE:

Ol Doinyo Lengai, Tanzania
The unique make-up of the lava from this mountain means it is as runny as water, and can stream out like a garden hose. It also allows the lava to erupt at temperatures of just 480–590°C (900–1090°F).

ABOVE:

Ol Doinyo Lengai, Tanzania
The temperature the lava erupts
at at Ol Doinyo Lengai is so
low that the lava can look
black in sunlight rather than
the typical glowing orange of
most lavas, and when it cools
it appears white. A night-time
eruption in 2004, however,
allowed the more natural
colour of the lava to shine
through.

RIGHT:

Ol Doinyo Lengai, Tanzania
Ol Doinyo Lengai varies
between eruptions of liquid
lava that form lava lakes and
fountains (known as effusive
eruptions) and explosive
eruptions that create large cinder
and ash cones. An episode of
the latter type in 2007 spewed
ash thousands of metres into
the air, which also fell on the
surrounding countryside, forcing
local residents to flee with their
livestock. Explosive eruptions
continued into 2008, building
a cone over 100m (330ft)
high that encircled a steep-sided
crater.

Muhavura, Uganda/Rwanda
At the easternmost end of the eight major volcanoes that make up the Virunga Mountains, of which Nyiragongo is a part, lies the extinct volcano Muhavura (left), on the border between Uganda and Rwanda. To its right can be seen the flatter-topped Gahinga. Muhavura is more than 4127m (13,540ft) high, and its crater is filled by a lake. The volcano forms part of the Virunga National Park, which is the home of the critically endangered mountain gorilla.

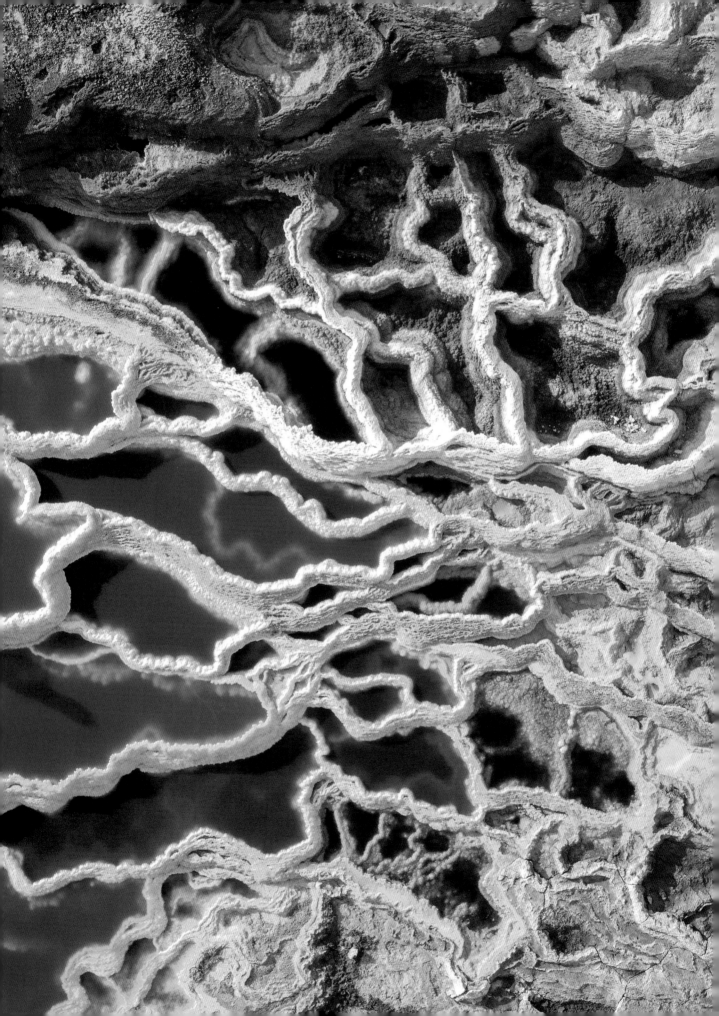

LEFT:

Dallol, Danakil Depression, Ethiopia

The divergence of three tectonic plates at the Horn of Africa created the sunken land of the Danakil Depression, home to the uniquely acidic hydrothermal system of Dallol. The tectonic activity also resulted in veins of magma running through the area as the land pulls apart, and birthed the Dallol volcano in 1926, the world's lowest surface volcano at -45m (-157ft).

ABOVE:

Dallol, Danakil Depression, Ethiopia

The hydrothermal fields are created by magma heating groundwater, which brings salt, minerals and acidic gases to the surface through hot springs. The brine reacts with the dissolved minerals, such as iron, potassium and sulphur, and, as the liquid evaporates in the hot, dry climate, extensive salt crystal formations in dazzling colours are left behind.

Erta Ale, Afar Depression, Ethiopia
Erta Ale is a continuously active basaltic shield volcano lying in the
Afar Depression (also known as the Afar Triangle), a sunken area of
land – of which the Danakil Depression is the northern part – caused
by the triple junction of three diverging tectonic plates. These three
plates are the Arabian plate and the Nubian and Somalian plates, the
latter two being part of the African plate that is fracturing along the
East African Rift, over which Erta Ale sits and which is responsible
for the volcano's supply of magma. Erta Ale has one and sometimes
two active lava lakes, one of only eight volcanoes in the world with
such a feature.

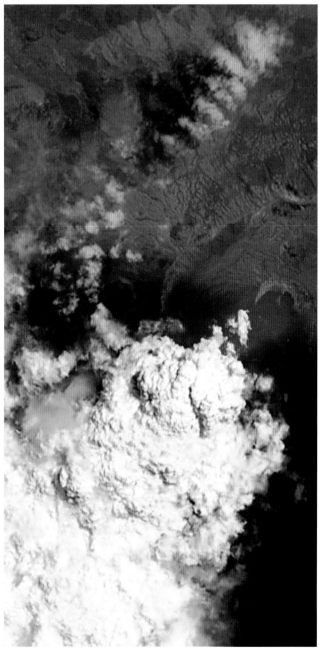

LEFT:

Erta Ale, Afar Depression, Ethiopia

Erta Ale has been erupting since 1967 and its name means 'smoking mountain' in the local Afar language. Its lava lake is thought to be longest lived in the world, having been present since the early twentieth century.

ABOVE:

Nabro, Danakil Depression, Eritrea

Visible and infrared light capture the heat from the 2011 eruption of Nabro, until then thought to be extinct. Ash glows above the vent. To its west is an active lava flow that cools to black while, above, escaping water condenses into a cloud.

Zendan-e Soleyman, West Azerbaijan province, Iran
The hollow cone of Zendan-e Soleyman is a 107m- (351ft) tall ancient extinct volcano formed of mostly calcium sediments, with the remains of various temple buildings surrounding the peak. Its crater, 65m (213ft) wide and 85m (279ft) deep, was filled with water centuries ago but has long sinced dried up. The mountain takes its name – 'the Prison of Solomon' – from the biblical king Solomon, after a local legend that tells how the Hebrew king imprisoned monsters within the mountain's deep cone.

Taftan, Sistan and Baluchestan province, Iran
Taftan is a stratovolcano on the Baluchestan Volcanic Arc, formed from the subduction of the oceanic Arabian plate beneath Iran at the Makran trench in the Gulf of Oman. The last verifiable lava flow at Taftan occurred around 7000 years ago, but reports of smoke over the last century and the constant fumarole activity around the crater, which belches out steam and sulphur, suggest the volcano is not dormant yet.

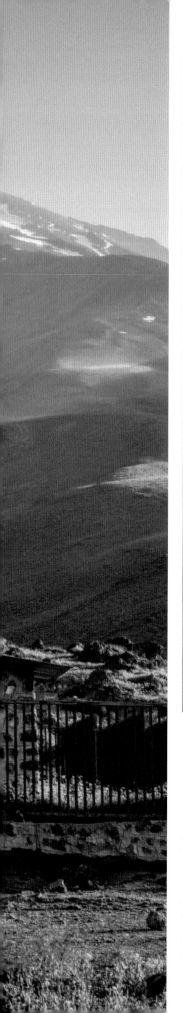

LEFT:

Mount Damavand, Iran

Mount Damavand, Asia's highest volcano, first erupted almost 1.78 million years ago in the Pleistocene. After a number of eruptions around 600,000 and 280,000 years ago, which helped create its steep cone of ash and lava flows, Damavand's last one was around 5300 BC. The volcano is topped by a small crater and there are adjacent fumaroles, hot springs and mineral deposits, which imply Damavand could be considered as a potentially active volcano.

ABOVE:

Mount Damavand, Iran

Damavand is steeped in Persian mythology and folklore. It is the symbol of Iranian resistance against despotism and foreign rule in Persian writings while Zoroastrianism relates how the three-headed dragon Azhi Dahaka was chained within the mountain until the end of the world. Damavand has also been named in the Iranian legend of Arash the archer as the location from which the hero shot his magical arrow to mark the border of Iran.

Asia, Pacific & Antarctica

Asia and the Pacific are home to the world's most spectacular volcanoes. This is due to their location along the fault lines collectively – although not officially – known as the Pacific Ring of Fire. This runs northeast from New Zealand, turns west through Papua New Guinea, Papua and Indonesia, then north, parallel to the Asian mainland along an arc that travels though the Philippines, Japan and Russia's Kamchatka Peninsula, before moving east and down the west coast of North America, through Central America and along the west side of South America. The ring is 'closed' by a few active and dormant volcanoes in Antarctica, although these are formed from the continent's own rift activity. In effect, this marks the entire boundaries of the Pacific Ocean.

The Ring of Fire is a result of the slow movement of tectonic plates. The Pacific Ocean plate is being forced under the surrounding continental plates all along its edges. Where the plates meet, magma bubbles up and volcanic activity ensues. The Ring of Fire has most of the world's earthquakes, including the largest, as well as the biggest and most violent volcanic eruptions we know of, including Krakatoa, Merapi and Pinatubo.

This chapter navigates the Asian, Pacific and Antarctic parts of the Ring of Fire, showcasing its variety, beauty and seemingly never-ending fury.

OPPOSITE:

Mutnovsky, Kamchatka Peninsula, Russia
Mutnovsky is one of the most active volcanoes on the Kamchatka Peninsula in the far east of Russia, which divides the Sea of Okhotsk and the Bering Sea in the North Pacific Ocean. It is a complex volcano formed of four merged stratovolcano cones and produces constant fumarole activity and rising columns of steam. Glacier ice melting above hot vents here can create boiling mud pools of different colours based on the mineral composition; this one contains deposits of sulphur.

LEFT:

Karymsky, Kamchatka Peninsula, Russia

Karymsky, a symmetrical stratovolcano, is currently the Kamchatka Peninusla's most active, having been in a constant cycle of eruption since 1996. The cone is decorated by lava flows that have occurred over the past 200 years.

ABOVE:

Kambalny, Kamchatka Peninsula, Russia

Kambalny's first major eruption in more than 600 years, in March 2017, saw mud streams and an ash plume that emerged from the mountain's western flank crater and rose up to 7km (4.35 miles) high, drifting up to 2000km (1243 miles) away.

Tolbachik, Kamchatka Peninsula, Russia
The Kamchatka Peninsula is an area of intense volcanic activity due to its position just to the northwest of the Kuril-Kamchatka Trench, part of the Ring of Fire, formed as a result of the subduction of the Pacific Ocean tectonic plate beneath the Okhotsk plate. There are 160 volcanoes on the peninsula, 29 of which are active, including Tolbachik. The mountain consists of two volcanoes, 'flat' Tolbachik (left) and 'sharp' Tolbachik (right), a flat-topped shield volcano and a peaked stratovolcano respectively.

Tolbachik, Kamchatka Peninsula, Russia
Tolbachik erupted in November 2012, with relatively fast-flowing basaltic lava streaming from two fissures and travelling up to 20km (12.4 miles) away. Ash plumes rose to maximum heights of 4000–6100m (13,000–20,000ft) and drifted to deposit ash on settlements many kilometres away.

Tolbachik, Kamchatka Peninsula, Russia
By the beginning of January 2013, Tolbachik had unleashed 1 cubic km (0.24 cu miles) of lava, which produced spectacular lava plumes that fountained up to 200m (660ft) high, and birthed four new cinder cones above the main fissure. Volcanic gases mixed with water to produce bright, acidic pools.

Tolbachik, Kamchatka Peninsula, Russia
The 2012–13 eruption of Tolbachik followed a strikingly similar path to the volcano's 1975–76 eruption, which lasted for a year and a half. Then, the huge amount of ash and volcanic debris ejected several kilometres into the atmosphere fell on a nearby forest, destroying much of its vegetation.

OVERLEAF LEFT TOP:
Tolbachik, Kamchatka Peninsula, Russia
The cooling lava fields of the land around Tolbachik as the 2012–13 eruption came to an end in September 2013 after 10 months of lava flows and ash clouds, which had destroyed a volcano observatory and other nearby structures. It stood as possibly Kamchatka's largest basaltic eruption in historic times.

OVERLEAF LEFT BOTTOM:
Cherpuk, Kamchatka Peninsula, Russia
A lake formed by melting ice and rainwater lies at the centre of one of Cherpuk's two cinder cones. North and South Cherpuk, as they are known, are located to the southwest of the volcano Ichinsky, and comprise the largest monogenetic volcanoes of the Sredinny Range, which runs from the northeast to the southwest of Kamchatka Peninsula. Monogenetic volcanic fields are made of small volcanoes that erupt only once each.

OVERLEAF RIGHT:
Koryaksky, Kamchatka Peninsula, Russia
Near the base of Koryaksky volcano lies the city of Petropavlovsk-Kamchatskiy. Koryaksky has had three major eruptions in the past 10,000 years that generated massive lava flows. A 2008 eruption unleashed a plume of ash that rose 6000m (20,000ft) high. Because of the dangers of the volcano's proximity to a large population, it has been designated one of the world's 16 Decade Volcanoes along with neighbouring Avachinsky, seen in the background with Kozelsky.

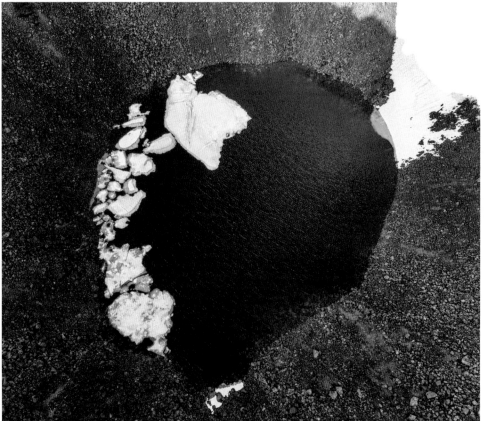

**Klyuchevskoy Sopka,
Kamchatka Peninsula, Russia**
Klyuchevskoy is a symmetrical
stratovolcano and the highest
mountain on the Kamchatka
Peninsula at 4754m (15,597ft),
as well as the highest
active volcano in Eurasia.
Klyuchevskoy is thought to have
first appeared around 6000
years ago and, similar to other
volcanoes in the region, it has
been almost continuously active
ever since. Weak eruptions in
2012 and 2013 were related to
the concurrent eruptions of such
nearby volcanoes as Tolbachik
and Karymsky.

**Gorely, Kamchatka Peninsula,
Russia**
A glacier occupies the base
of the West crater of Gorely,
formed during a 1984–86
eruption. The glacier is also
a riverhead that flows into
the northwest part of the
caldera and descends in a series
of waterfalls. Gorely itself
formed in the caldera
of a much older shield volcano,
and is a ridge of overlapping
craters that cover 150 square
km (58 sq miles).

**Avachinsky, Kamchatka
Peninsula, Russia**
A Decade Volcano along with
Koryaksky, Avachinsky has
erupted 16 times since 1737,
and most violently in 1945,
when 0.25 cubic km (0.06 cu
miles) were ejected. Eruptions
are usually explosive, with
pyroclastic flows and lahars
– a violent type of mud or
debris flow from a volcano,
composed of a mix of
pyroclastic material, rocky
debris and water. It is one
of the most active volcanoes on
the peninsula.

RIGHT:
Kamen, Kamchatka Peninsula, Russia
Lenticular clouds hover over the peak of Kamen, and wreath the neck of Klyuchevskoy behind it. Kamen is a dormant stratovolcano and the second highest of the peninsula.

OVERLEAF:
Paektu, Jilin Province, China/ Ryanggang Province, North Korea
Known as Changbai in China, Paektu, on the China–North Korea border, is an active volcano with a caldera containing Heaven Lake. The lake has been recognized as the highest volcanic lake in the world, while a nearby waterfall, which plunges 68m (223ft) over a cliff, is the largest waterfall originating from a crater lake. The caldera was formed in an AD 946 eruption, one of the most violent of the last 5000 years.

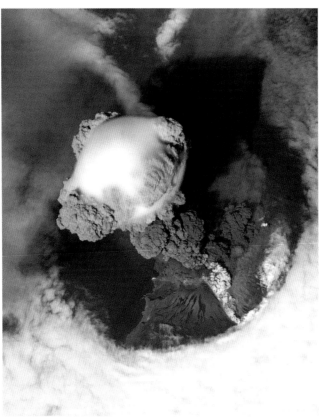

FAR LEFT:

Komezuka, Aso, Kyushu, Japan

In the crater of Aso, one of the world's largest calderas, sits the 50m (164ft) Komezuka, called the cutest volcano in Japan. Its name means 'rice bowl' in reference to its shape. Bright green grass covers both the cone and surrounding fields during the spring and summer months.

LEFT TOP:

Sarychev Peak, Matua Island, Kuril Islands

A view from the International Space Station of the eruption of Sarychev Peak in June 2009. A hole in the overhead clouds, possibly caused by the shock wave from the explosion, allowed astronauts to take a clear picture of the ash plume and the white cloud of pyroclastic flow descending the right side of the volcano, some of which ultimately reached the sea. A cap-like pileus cloud is visible on top of the rising column. A pileus is a lenticular cloud that forms above severe developing weather, including rising clouds from volcanoes.

LEFT BOTTOM:

Mount Fuji, Honshu, Japan

Mount Fuji is an active stratovolcano composed of three successive volcanoes and last erupted in 1707–08. It is located at a triple junction trench where the Amurian, Okhotsk and Philippine Sea plates meet. The Pacific plate is being subducted beneath these plates, resulting in volcanic activity.

Mount Fuji, Honshu, Japan
Due to Fuji's near perfect
symmetrical tapered shape,
snow-topped for around five
months a year, the mountain
is a sacred symbol of Japan
and holds a special place in
Japanese culture. Its image
has been used in the country's
artistic output and mentioned in
literature countless times over
the centuries.

LEFT TOP:

Mount Aso, Kyushu, Japan
The central cone group of Mount Aso contains five peaks, including Mount Naka (pictured), an active volcano that continuously emits smoke and has occasional eruptions. Aso's very large caldera formed from four major eruptive events between 270,000 and 90,000 years ago. As large amounts of pyroclastic flow and volcanic ash were emitted from the volcanic chamber, it collapsed to form the huge caldera. The pyroclastic flow of the fourth and largest eruption is believed to have covered half of Kyushu and even reached a part of Honshu.

LEFT MIDDLE:

Mayon, Bicol Region, Luzon, Philippines
Eruptions of Mayon range from Strombolian to Plinian in nature, and lava flows, pyroclastic flows and mud flows have in the past devastated lowland settlements. Mayon's most violent recorded eruption, in 1814, killed more than 1200 people, laid waste to several towns and may have contributed to the 'Year without a Summer' of 1816, when average global temperatures dropped by 0.4–0.7°C (0.72–1.3°F).

LEFT BOTTOM:

Mayon, Bicol Region, Luzon, Philippines
Mayon is considered one of the world's most perfectly formed volcanoes because of its nearly symmetrical conical shape. This is the result of eruptions occurring from the single central conduit that emerges at its peak.

OPPOSITE:

Mount Chokai, Yuza, Honshu, Japan
Chokai is an isolated complex stratovolcano formed of older and newer volcanoes, and is topographically unique in that it rises directly from the sea to an altitude of 2236m (7336ft). Chokai's ecosystem is also unique, owing to the fact the volcano has the highest amount of precipitation of any Japanese mountain.

Mayon, Bicol Region, Luzon, Philippines
Mayon is a stratovolcano with a small central summit crater. It is the most active volcano in the Philippines and has had numerous eruptions of different strengths in the last 500 years, including in January 2018 (pictured), which saw lava fountains, lava bombs, ash clouds and pyroclastic flows.

Mount Pinatubo, Zambales Mountains, Luzon, Philippines
Prior to a 1991 eruption, not much was known about Pinatubo. That all changed in June of that year as the second-largest terrestrial eruption of the twentieth century began. Ash and huge pyroclastic flows buried valleys, an ash cloud was blown around the globe and the simultaneous Typhoon Yunya brought flooding lahars (pictured), destroying infrastructure and altering river sytems. The eruption ejected roughly 10 cubic km (2.4 cu miles) of magma and 20 million tonnes (22 million tons) of sulphur dioxide.
The gases emitted led to global temperatures dropping by about 0.5°C (0.9°F) over the following two years and reduced the density of the ozone layer.

OPPOSITE TOP:

Mount Pinatubo, Zambales Mountains, Luzon, Philippines
So much magma was ejected in the 1991 eruption that the summit collapsed to create a caldera. Annual monsoons soon filled the crater to form Lake Pinatubo, which was initially highly acidic and very warm. Further rains cooled and diluted the waters, reducing its acidity and swallowing a new lava dome formed in 1992.

OPPOSITE BOTTOM:

Mount Rinjani, Lombok, Indonesia
Mount Rinjani, at 3726m (12,224ft), is the second highest volcano in Indonesia. Its caldera was formed by the 1257 eruption of Samalas in one of the largest volcanic events since the end of the last ice age 11,500 years ago, and which may have triggered a period of global cooling and failed harvests. Rinjani's caldera is filled by Segara Anak lake, which itself saw the emergence of a cone now known as Gunung Baru Jari in 1994 and 1995 eruptions, the lava from subsequent eruptions of which has filled a part of the lake.

RIGHT:

Chu Dang Ya, Gia Lai province, Vietnam

The ancient extinct volcano of Chu Dang Ya, meaning 'wild ginger root' in the J'rai language, still shows the legacy of its volcanism in the red tint of basalt soil evident in many of the fields that now carpet the volcano. Despite no water filling the crater or any irrigation setup, the trees and fields, covered in the green of the taro and sweet potato fields, remain verdant because of the blessings of the monsoon.

OVERLEAF:

Kelimutu, Flores, Indonesia

Kelimutu is known for its lakes of ever-changing colours. The colours come from the different minerals in the water, and the balance between rainfall and gas input from the volcano. Each lake has its own unique gas input so colours change idependently.

**Anak Krakatoa, Krakatoa
Archipelago, Sunda Strait,
Indonesia**

The Krakatoa Archipelago was
formed and reshaped many times
by Krakatoa's volcanism, most
famously during the volcano's
1883 eruption, which destroyed
70 per cent of Krakatoa island
and its archipelago as the volcano
collapsed to form a caldera.

**Anak Krakatoa, Krakatoa
Archipelago, Sunda Strait,
Indonesia**

The 1883 eruption of Krakatoa
was one of the most violent in
recorded history. The ash fall and
explosions causing pyroclastic
flows that triggered tsunamis
killed at least 36,000 people. In
1927, Anak Krakatoa (pictured)
emerged from the caldera to
join the three islands left after
the eruption. It has exhibited
sporadic and destructive activity
for decades, notably in 2018.

**Anak Krakatoa, Krakatoa
Archipelago, Sunda Strait,
Indonesia**

The third of the four major
explosions of the 1883 Krakatoa
eruption was heard as far as
4780km (2970 miles) away,
with its pressure wave travelling
around the earth a number of
times. This was said to have
burst the eardrums of sailors
64km (40 miles) away. Bodies
were washing up on the shores of
East Africa up to a year later.

**Mount Sinabung,
Sumatra, Indonesia**
Mount Sinabung is a
stratovolcano that had, until
sporadic eruptions started in
2010, been dormant for 400
years. It lies on the Sunda Arc,
a volcanic arc that produced
such islands as Sumatra and Java,
created by the subduction of the
Indo-Australian plate under the
Eurasian plate.

**Mount Sinabung,
Sumatra, Indonesia**
In January 2014, Sinabung
erupted once more, sending
a 4000m (13,000ft) high
cloud of ash into the sky, which
damaged property and crops
and poisoned animals. Amid
the ash columns and cascading
pyroclastic flows, volcanic
lightning forked the air. This is
created by the build-up of charge
during the collision of volcanic
ash particles, rock fragments
and sometimesice formed from
rapidly rising moist air. The
updrafts separate the charged
areas, causing the breakdown of
static electricity into lightning.

Mount Merapi, Java, Indonesia
Mount Merapi is the most active volcano in Indonesia and has erupted
regularly in the last 500 years. Because it is only 28km (17 miles)
from Yogyakarta city and its population of 2.4 million, and villages
dot the mountainside as high as 1700m (5600ft) up, Merapi has been
designated one of the world's Decade Volcanoes due to the danger it
poses to people and property.

LEFT TOP:

2010 eruption of Mount Merapi, Magelang, Java, Indonesia
A house in Magelang in Central Java, which was hit by a pyroclastic flow from the eruption of Mount Merapi, 14km (8.7 miles) away, in October 2010. More than 350,000 people were evacuated from their homes during the month-long eruption, but some returned or stayed, which contributed to the death toll of 353, mostly due to pyroclastic flows.

LEFT BOTTOM:

Mount Merapi, Java, Indonesia
The rising lava dome of Merapi spills magma over its edge to trickle down the mountain and threaten whatever it finds. Lava domes are mounds built of magma that is so thick that it allows lava to flow only slowly and thus the mound to rise. This is because of high silica content or low gas content in the magma.

OPPOSITE:

Mount Merapi, Java, Indonesia
Merapi's 2010 eruption ejected huge eruption columns – clouds of super-heated ash and tephra rising on expanding steam and volcanic gases. When the rising, expanding cloud reaches a height where it is too dense to be lifted by convection or momentum, it falls to earth to form pyroclastic flows or surges.

LEFT:

2010 eruption of Mount Merapi, Java, Indonesia
This village was covered in falling ash from the 2010 eruption of Merapi. In some places, the ash piled up 30cm (12in) deep.

ABOVE TOP:

Mount Merapi destruction, Java, Indonesia
The village of Balerante looked like a ghost village after the effects of falling ash and incandescent material ejected by Mount Merapi.

ABOVE BOTTOM:

Mount Merapi destruction, Java, Indonesia
Another house and its contents burnt and destroyed by the violent output of Merapi in 2010. Volcanic bombs and hot clouds of ash, gas and steam, with temperatures up to 800°C (1500°F), had spread over a distance of 10km (6 miles).

**Mounts Bromo, Batok
and Semeru, Bromo
Tengger Semeru National Park,
Java, Indonesia**
In the middle of a sand sea lies
the Tengger massif, comprising
Mount Bromo (bottom
left), Mount Batok (middle
foreground) and three other
volcanoes. These all formed
within the caldera of an older
volcano, Tengger, and are all
still active apart from Batok.
Mount Semeru, the highest peak
in Java, and part of the Semeru
or Jambangan Group, stands
in the middle background.

Mount Bromo erupting,
Tengger Semeru National Park, Java, Indonesia
The smoke pouring from the crater of Mount Bromo is whipped away over the sand sea by the wind towards some of Java's air corridors, raising the potential of damage to aircraft. Ingestion of ash can stop engines because the heat of the turbines can melt the ash, which can form a glass coating on the turbine blades. Ash can also sandblast cockpit windows and contaminate fuel.

LEFT:

The Nut, Stanley,
Tasmania, Australia
The Nut, a 143m (469ft) high, sheer-sided bluff that juts into the Bass Strait, is all that remains of an ancient volcano, active between 70 and 25 million years ago. The leftover stump is what was once a lava lake in the volcano's crater, which cooled and solidified. Over time, weathering and erosion removed the weaker volcanic fragments that formed the cone to leave the hard basalt of the lava pool on its own as a conspicuous marker of earlier volcanism.

Manam, Manam Island, Papua New Guinea

In the southwest portion of the Pacific Ring of Fire, where the Pacific plate sinks beneath the Indo-Australian plate, lies the submerged volcano Manam, one of the region's most active, its top forming a 10km (6 miles) wide island 13km (8 miles) off Papua New Guinea. The volcano has erupted frequently since its first recorded eruption in 1616, with recurring low-level ash plumes, occasional Strombolian activity, lava flows, pyroclastic avalanches and large ash plumes from its two active summit craters. It is currently in an eruptive cycle that began in 2014.

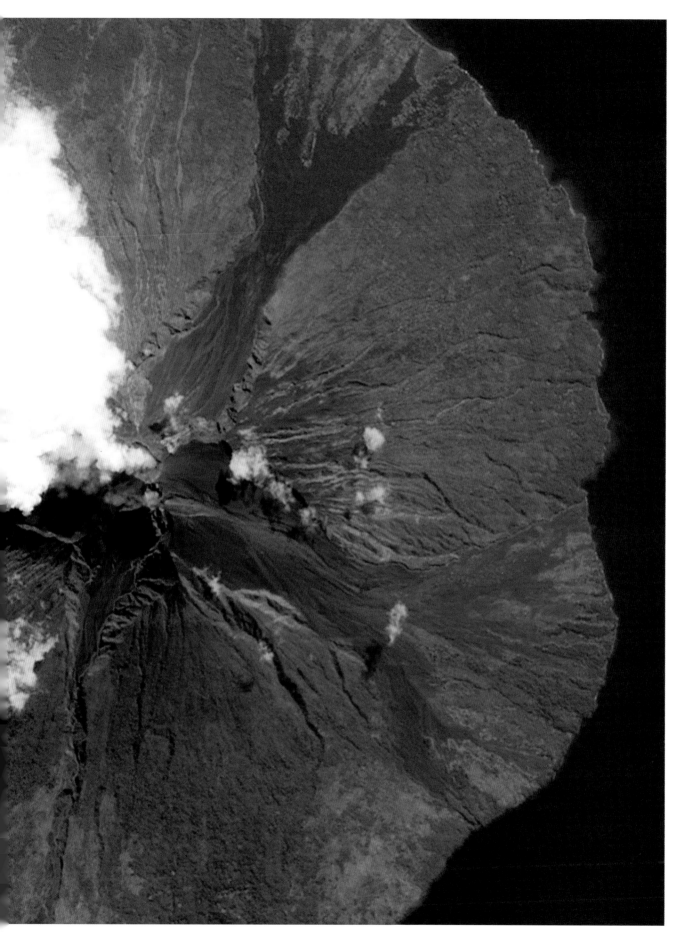

Volcanic lakes of Mount Tongariro, Tongariro National Park, North Island, New Zealand
Mount Tongariro is a complex volcano and is, with three other volcanoes, part of a volcanic centre in the Taupo Volcanic Zone that has been active for 2 million years. Tongariro itself is made of layers of lava and tephra and first erupted 275,000 years ago.

ABOVE:

White Island, Bay of Plenty, New Zealand

Also known as Whakaari, this stratovolcano is 48km (30 miles) from the east coast of New Zealand's North Island and is the peak of a much larger submarine volcano. The amphitheatre-shaped active crater is open to the southeast after major flank landslides, where the open sea breaches it in three places.

RIGHT:

White Island, Bay of Plenty, New Zealand

Whakaari, lying at the northern end of the Taupo Volcanic Zone, consists of two overlapping cones, one of which is extinct and partially eroded. It has been built up by continuous activity over the last 150,000 years, and has been emitting gas at least since Captain Cook saw it in 1769. It also underwent possibly the world's longest known eruption, from December 1975 to September 2000.

OPPOSITE:

Mount Ngauruhoe, Tongariro National Park, North Island, New Zealand

While often regarded as a separate mountain, Ngauruhoe (behind the central crater) is geologically a cone of Mount Tongariro, and is its youngest and most active vent in the Tongariro volcanic complex.

ABOVE TOP:
Mount Ruapehu, Tongariro National Park, North Island, New Zealand
Mount Ruapehu is an active stratovolcano at the southern end of the Taupo Volcanic Zone and is New Zealand's largest active volcano. It began erupting 250,000 years ago. Some scenes of the fictional Mordor and Mount Doom in Peter Jackson's *The Lord of the Rings* films were filmed on the slopes of Mount Ruapehu.

ABOVE BOTTOM:
Mawson Peak, Heard Island, Australia
An Australian territory in the far south of the Indian Ocean, but more closely connected to Antarctica, 1600km (1000 miles) south, Heard Island is one of the most remote places on earth. It is home to Mawson Peak, which, at 2745m (9006ft), is higher than any summit on the Australian mainland and is one of the country's two active volcanoes.

RIGHT:
Mount Ruapehu, Tongariro National Park, North Island, New Zealand
A series of very explosive Plinian eruptions occurred at Ruapehu between about 22,600 and 10,000 years ago. Since then, only one vent has probably been active, at Crater Lake in the summit region. Major eruptions in historic times seem to occur every 50 years, with the lake filling with warm, acidic water in between.

Mount Discovery, Antarctica
Mount Discovery is an extinct
volcano 2681m (8796ft)
high situated at the head
of McMurdo Sound and
overlooking Ross Ice Shelf.
Extending out from Mount
Discovery and into the ice shelf
like a long, hooked tenatacle
is Minna Bluff (pictured). The
volcano was discovered by
Captain Scott's British National
Antarctic Expedition of
1901–04, and named after their
expedition ship, *Discovery*.

ABOVE:

Brown Bluff, Tabarin Peninsula, Antarctica

Brown Bluff is a tuya formed in the last million years from subglacial eruptions in a glacial lake. Tuyas are flat-topped, steep-sided cones made in a process that begins with lava erupting under a thick glacier. The ice cools the lava very quickly so it cannot travel far, leaving it to pile up into a steep-sided hill. If the eruption continues, lava can emerge through the top of the ice to create normal-looking flows that produce a flat cap on top of the hill. Tuyas are rare, and are restricted to regions that were covered by glaciers and had active volcanism at the same time.

OPPOSITE:

Mount Erebus, Ross Island, Antarctica

Mount Erebus is both the most active and the second highest volcano in Antarctica (after Mount Sidley) and the southernmost active volcano on earth. It lies on a volcanic hotspot (regions where the underlying mantle is unusually hot) responsible for the high volcanic activity on Ross Island. Erebus has erupted continuously since its discovery in 1841 and is one of the few volcanoes on the planet to have an active lava lake.

North America & Caribbean

THE COLLISION of the North American tectonic plate with the Pacific plate creates the northeastern part of the Pacific Ring of Fire, which snakes its way down the west coast of North America. The volcanic chain here comprises the northern section of the American Cordillera, a series of mountain ranges that make up the western backbone of North, Central and South America.

This northern portion, the North American Cordillera, features some of the most prominent volcanoes on that continent, and runs from Alaska to Canada and California to Mexico.

At the same time as the North American plate collides with the Pacific plate, it also rubs up against the Caribbean plate. South American oceanic crust also subducts under the latter, causing the Caribbean's volcanic activity.

There are 169 potentially active volcanoes in the USA, most of which are in Alaska's Aleutian island chain. Whereas North America's volcanoes are known for their explosive natures, Hawaii's are gently sloping shield volcanoes formed from slow lava flows.

This chapter considers some of the most famous and most active volcanoes in the world, including Mount St Helens in Washington, USA, and Hawaii's Kilauea, and highlights the devastating effects of an eruption on the local landscape and people.

LEFT:
Mount Shasta, California, USA
A dramatic cloud formation hovers over Mount Shasta. The volcano is at the southern end of the Cascade Range, a chain of mountains that runs from British Columbia in Canada through Washington and Oregon to northern California. Shasta is formed of four overlapping volcanic cones, and is the most voluminous in the Cascade Volcanic Arc.

Augustine, Cook Inlet, Alaska, USA
Augustine's major eruptions usually begin with vent-clearing explosions, and are then followed by more low-key effusions of lava. There have been large eruptions in 1883, 1935, 1963–64, 1976, 1986 and 2006. The 1986 episode (pictured) deposited ash over Anchorage and disrupted air traffic in south-central Alaska.

LEFT:

Mount Shishaldin, Unimak Island, Aleutian Islands, Alaska, USA

A view of the interior of the small, 150m (490ft) crater of Mount Shishaldin. The modern volcano was formed less than 10,000 years ago on top of an older one eroded by glacial movement, the remnants of which can be seen on the west and northeast sides of the newer volcano. Shishaldin also has more than two dozen pyroclastic cones dotting its northwest flank, which is covered by massive lava flows.

ABOVE TOP:

Augustine, Cook Inlet, Alaska, USA

The numerous eruptions of the Augustine volcano have birthed an island of the same name in Cook Inlet, Alaska. The volcano consists of a central complex of several overlapping lava domes and lava flows, surrounded by pyroclastic, lahar, ash debris and avalanche fragments from past dome collapses.

ABOVE BOTTOM:

Mount Shishaldin, Unimak Island, Aleutian Islands, Alaska, USA

The most symmetrical cone-shaped, glacier-clad large mountain on Earth, the volcano's contour lines are nearly perfect circles above 2000m (6500ft), where the mountain is almost always covered by glacial snow and ice. Mount Shishaldin's summit crater gives off an almost constant plume of steam, and frequent explosive activity, primarily consisting of Strombolian ash eruptions from the summit crater, as well as occasional lava flows, has been recorded since the eighteenth century.

Anahim Peak, British Columbia, Canada
Anahim Peak is a volcanic cone sitting on the northeast flank of the Rainbow Range, an extinct shield volcano. Both, along with two other shield volcanoes known as the Ilgachuz and Itcha Ranges, are part of the Anahim Volcanic Belt, which is believed to have formed as a result of the North American plate sliding westward over a long-lived center of upwelling magma called the Anahim hotspot. This hotspot is thought to be similar to the one feeding the Hawaiian Islands.

Mount Si, Washington, USA
Mount Si lies on the western edge of the Cascade Range, a mix of volcanoes and mountains, and represents what is left of a volcano formed from the subduction of the oceanic plate. Mount Si looms large over the town of North Bend, and both gained fame through their featuring in the American 1990s mystery drama *Twin Peaks*. The mountain is one of the most popular destinations for hikers in the area, with 80,000–100,000 visiting annually.

Mount St Helens, Washington, USA
Mount St Helens is an active stratovolcano in the Cascade Range and is a part of the Cascade Volcanic Arc, a portion of the Pacific Ring of Fire. The arc was formed by the subduction of small, eastward-moving tectonic plates, the remnants of an ancient oceanic plate, beneath the southwestward-moving North American plate. This tectonic activity triggered the volcanism of the Cascades and was responsibile for the 1980 eruption of Mount St Helens, one of the most notorious eruptions of recent times.

Mount St Helens, Washington, USA
The eruption of Mount St Helens in 1980 was the deadliest and most financially devastating volcanic event in US history, killing 57 people and costing $1.1 billion in property and infrastructure damage. For almost two months, eruptions of steam, ash plumes and thousands of earthquakes heralded something larger. When it came, the results were unprecedented. A landslide was followed by a blast of superheated gas, ash and pumice that flew over the surrounding land at up to supersonic speed, obliterating, scything down or burning 600 square km (230 sq miles) of forest.

Mount St Helens, Washington, USA
The landslide that preceded and triggered the blast of
pyroclastic material in the 1980 eruption was caused by the
collapse of the entire north face of the mountain after an
earthquake, and carried with it debris that covered an area of
62 square km (24 sq miles) with many metres of rubble. It was
the largest landslide in recorded history and left a clear view
into the volcano's crater for the first time.

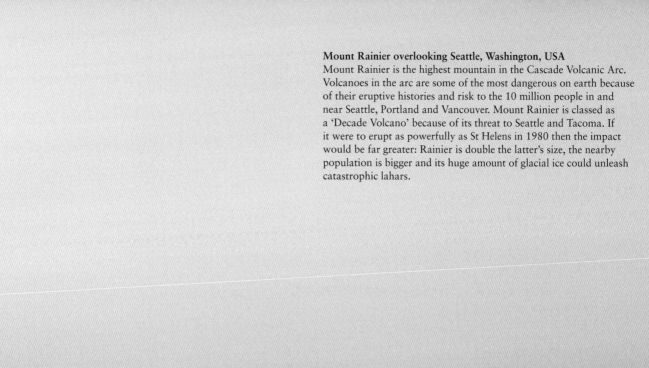

Mount Rainier overlooking Seattle, Washington, USA
Mount Rainier is the highest mountain in the Cascade Volcanic Arc. Volcanoes in the arc are some of the most dangerous on earth because of their eruptive histories and risk to the 10 million people in and near Seattle, Portland and Vancouver. Mount Rainier is classed as a 'Decade Volcano' because of its threat to Seattle and Tacoma. If it were to erupt as powerfully as St Helens in 1980 then the impact would be far greater: Rainier is double the latter's size, the nearby population is bigger and its huge amount of glacial ice could unleash catastrophic lahars.

**Mount Adams,
Washington, USA**
Around 55km (34 miles) east
of Mount St Helens is Mount
Adams, also in the Cascade
Range and part of the same
volcanic arc. Although it has not
erupted for a millennium, it is
not considered extinct. Mount
Adams' flat top was formed
through lava extrusions from
separate vents, and the rest of its
profile from a series of individual
eruptions of lava that, over time,
created numerous overlapping
cones. The first of this series of
eruptions was 500,000 years ago,
and each stage was punctuated
by a long period of dormancy.

Mount Hood, Oregon, USA
Mount Hood is part of the
Cascade Range, formed from
the magma generated by the
subduction process of the oceanic
crust beneath North America
being forced up to the surface.
While hot springs and steam
vents are still active on Mount
Hood, its last major eruption was
200 years ago and the volcano
is considered dormant. Separate
phases of eruptive activity
produced pyroclastic flows
and lahars that carried erupted
materials down all of its major
rivers. Grey volcanic deposits
extend southwards along the
banks of the White River (see
lower left).

Mount Hood, Oregon, USA
Mount Hood is a typically cone-
shaped stratovolcano formed by
layered lava flows and explosive
eruption deposits, and hosts 12
glaciers along its upper flanks.
Similar to other glaciers in the
Pacific Northwest, those on
Mount Hood have been receding
due to global warming, and have
lost an estimated 61 per cent
of their volume over the past
century. The predicted loss of
glacial meltwater on the current
warming trajectory will have
significant effects on regional
hydrology as well as water
supplies.

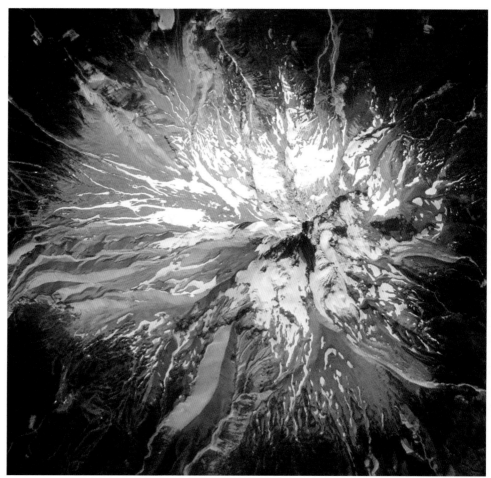

Crater Lake, Oregon, USA

Crater Lake, famed for its beautiful deep blue colour and the unrivalled clarity of its waters, fills the caldera of Mount Mazama on the Cascade Volcanic Arc, which collapsed following a massive eruption 7700 years ago. No rivers feed the lake so it took around 720 years for just rainwater and snowmelt to fill the caldera to its present depth of 594m (1949ft), which makes it the deepest lake in the USA. Later volcanic activity saw the formation of Wizard Island, a small cinder cone within the 8 × 9.7km (5 × 6 miles) wide lake. There is some hydrothermal activity along the lake floor, suggesting that, at some time in the future, Mazama may erupt once more.

ALL PHOTOGRAPHS:

Devils Tower, Wyoming, USA

Considered sacred by Northern Plains Indians and indigenous groups, 264m (867ft) high Devils Tower is an unusual geological feature that protrudes out of the prairie surrounding the Black Hills. It is thought to have been formed by an intrusion of magma into surrounding sedimentary rock and would only have become a visible landmark when all the sedimentary material eroded away. Some believe, however, that Devils Tower is all that remains of what was once a huge explosive volcano. The Tower became a lot more famous after its appearance in Steven Spielberg's *Close Encounters of the Third Kind*.

Lassen Volcanic National Park, California, USA
The undulating, red-blotched Painted Dunes of Lassen Volcanic National Park are a unique feature of the landscape of this area, for which the park's many volcanoes are responsible. The dunes are, in fact, pumice fields that formed from layers of volcanic ash, which became so vividly oxidized (and therefore colourful) because it fell on top of a bed of lava flows while they were still hot. The dunes lie beneath Cinder Cone, an almost perfectly symmetrical cinder cone, one of four types of volcanoes in the park – along with stratovolcanoes, shield volcanoes and lava (or plug) domes – one of the only places in the world where all four types can be seen in one place. The volcanoes here are part of the most recently active Lassen volcanic centre, which began to erupt about 825,000 years ago.

Lassen Peak, Lassen Volcanic National Park, California, USA
Lassen Peak is the dominant feature in the park and is the southernmost volcano in the Cascade Range. Part of the Cascade Volcanic Arc, Lassen Peak is a lava dome formed from the slow build-up of thick lava and, with a volume of 2.5 cubic km (0.6 cu miles), is the largest lava dome in the world. In 1915, a powerful eruption from the volcano devastated the area, and spread ash as far as 450km (280 miles) to the east, making it the only volcano, along with Mount St Helens, in mainland USA to erupt in the twentieth century. While the area around Lassen Peak sleeps now, steam vents, boiling springs, and bubbling mudpots remain active, indicating that the volcanic centre still smoulders.

Black Butte, Mount Shasta, California, USA
Black Butte is a cluster of overlapping lava domes and is a satellite cone of Mount Shasta. The lava domes were created at the foot of Shastina, following a period of its major eruptions around 9500 years ago. These eruptions were typical of lava domes, with magma so thick and stiff it did not form a lava flow. Rather, it cooled into angular blocks after it was slowly squeezed out of the vents and rolled down the slope as rocks, which led to the formation of the steep, rocky sides of Black Butte.

Cinder Cone, Lassen Volcanic National Park, California, USA
The cone is 213m (699ft) high and formed of loose scoria (dark, pitted volcanic rock) from five lava flows from eruptions in the 1650s, as well as an earlier cone. This earlier cone was mostly destroyed by lava flows at its base, on which pieces of red, cemented scoria were carried away to form the Painted Dunes. A cinder cone is made of a pile-up of solidified loose ash and cinders from explosions or lava fountains in a single eruption, after which the vent ceases activity forever.

San Francisco Peaks, Coconino National Forest, Arizona, USA
The San Francisco Peaks are a volcanic mountain range and a remnant of an eroded stratovolcano complex, San Francisco Mountain. The range is part of the San Francisco volcanic field, which covers 4700 square km (1800 sq miles) of the southern boundary of the Colorado Plateau, and contains 600 volcanoes ranging in age from nearly 6 million to less than 1000 years old. The volcanic field formed from the movement of the North American plate over a geological hotspot of unusually hot mantle.

Haleakala, Maui, Hawaiian Islands, USA
Haleakala, also known as the East Maui Volcano, is a massive shield volcano that makes up more than 75 per cent of the island of Maui. The western 25 per cent is formed by another volcano, Mauna Kahalawai. The tallest peak of Haleakala (meaning 'house of the sun'), at 3005m (10,023ft), is Pu'u 'Ula'ula, from where one looks down into a massive depression, the interior of which is dotted with volcanic cones.

ABOVE:
Haleakala, Maui,
Hawaiian Islands, USA
Close-ups of the cinder cones that decorate the crater floor of Haleakala. Unusually, the crater is not, in fact, volcanic in origin, and is therefore not a crater at all; nor is it a caldera created by a massive summit collapse after an eruption. Instead it was formed by two separate parts of the volcano falling into each other at the summit and merging to create a valley. Subsequent eruptions formed the cinder cones seen on the crater floor.

RIGHT TOP:
Mount Kilauea, Hawaii,
Hawaiian Islands, USA
Lava flows from Kilauea pour into the ocean at Hilo. Kilauea sits above the Hawaiian volcanic hotspot and is the eruptive centre of the Hawaiian–Emperor seamount chain, a mostly underwater mountain range. It has two active rift zones and erupted continuously from 1983 to 2018, with lava flowing all the way to the ocean to create new land.

RIGHT BOTTOM:
Mount Kilauea, Hawaii,
Hawaiian Islands, USA
A ball of steam approximating the shape of a mushroom cloud rises up as lava from Kilauea enters the ocean on the island of Hawaii, the largest of the Hawaiian Islands. Kilauea is the most active of the five volcanoes that form the island and is 210,000–280,000 years old, having first emerged from the ocean 100,000 years ago.

Leilani Estates, 2018 eruption of Kilauea, Hawaii, Hawaiian Islands, USA

Lava from the 2018 lower Puna eruption of Kilauea creeps down a street in Leilani Estates. This was related to the larger eruption of Kilauea that began in 1983. Of the 24 fissure vents that formed during this eruption, 14 were active to varying extents within Leilani Estates. One of these saw lava fountaining as high as 100m (330ft) and its advancement had reached a speed of 76m/h (249ft/h) by the time it reached the sea, burying or covering major roads on its way. Lava flows also evaporated the largest natural freshwater lake in the Hawaiian Islands, partly or completely destroyed several towns, filled in Kapoho Bay and ultimately covered 35 square km (13.7 sq miles) of land. About 3.54 square km (1.37 sq miles) of new land was created in the ocean.

LEFT TOP:

Road 'resurfacing', Hawaii, Hawaiian Islands, USA

Lava flows from the long eruption of Kilauea, from 1983 to 2018, as well as earlier eruptions, have buried many roads on Hawaii; this is sometimes ironically referred to as a 'resurfacing' of the road. While some roads are left closed, others are kept open by taking action while the lava is still hot but not glowing. Gravel is thrown on to the lava to test how much material per square metre is required for the lava to become a practicable road while solidifying; soil is also analysed to search for air pockets that could warn of possible road collapses.

LEFT BOTTOM:

Lava fields, Hawaii, Hawaiian Islands, USA

The end of the Kilauea eruption irrevocably changed the landscape. The lava lake at Pu'u O'o crater, which formed in 1983 and was responsible for much of the lava flows during that eruption, collapsed to redirect lava elsewhere (such as Leilani Estates) in a last spasm of violence. Once the unchecked flow over land stops, however, it cools and solidifies to form seas of dark-coloured rock. While initially it seems a hellish landscape, it holds a unique attraction for tourists unaccustomed to the earth pouring out its innards on to its surface.

OPPOSITE:

2018 eruption of Kilauea, Hawaii, Hawaiian Islands, USA

The outbreaks of lava fountains, lava flows and volcanic gas in Leilani Estates during Kilauea's 2018 eruption were preceded by earthquakes and ground deformation that created cracks in the roads. These cracks were because of lava entering the ground beneath, distorting it. Other cracks in the area poured out steam and, later, lava.

Diamond Head, Oahu, Hawaiian Islands, USA
Diamond Head is a volcanic tuff or ash cone, a volcano born when magma boils water to steam to cause an explosion of ash, rock and volcanic bombs. The resulting pyroclastic material and eruption column fallout build the cone. Diamond Head is part of a stage of volcanism on the island that has created numerous cones and vents, and is about 400,000–500,000 years old.

Hanauma Bay and Koko Crater, Oahu, Hawaiian Islands, USA
About 32,000 years ago, the Honolulu volcanic series created the tuff ring of Hanauma Bay, breached by the ocean, and the somewhat taller tuff cone of Koko Crater (background). The Honolulu volcanic series birthed many other vents and cones, including Diamond Head, in a new volcanic field in this southeast portion of Oahu beginning around 500,000 years ago, and is a later stage of the volcanism that formed the now dormant, fragmented Ko'olau volcano.

ABOVE:

Popocatépetl, Izta-Popo Zoquiapan National Park, Mexico
Popocatépetl is a 730,000-year-old active stratovolcano located in
the states of Puebla, Morelos and Mexico, and is the second highest
peak in Mexico at 5426m (17,802ft). It has a twin, although dormant,
volcano called Iztaccihuatl, to which it is linked by the high saddle
Paso de Cortés. The volcano contains a steep-walled crater 400m ×
600m (1300ft × 2000ft) wide, from which smoke has been constantly
pouring since 1993, as well as ash, rocks and lava. It had been
dormant for about half a century before activity increased in 1991.
Popocatépetl has a long history of volcanism, having arisen from two
collapsed ancestral calderas.

OPPOSITE:

**San Juan Parangaricutiro, Parícutin Volcanic Field,
Michoacán, Mexico**
The village of San Juan Parangaricutiro has now been rebuilt after
its destruction in the sudden formation of nearby volcano Parícutin
in a farmer's cornfield in 1943. The devastation caused is clear to
see, with this church being one of the few remaining features after
the village's burial by ash and lava. It is now a popular tourist
attraction.

LEFT:

Parícutin, Michoacán, Mexico
Parícutin was formed on the northern flank of the Cerros de Tancítaro, which itself lies on top of an old shield volcano. By the end of its nine-year eruptive phase in 1952, Parícutin reached 424m (1391ft) above the valley floor. The cone is surrounded by old volcanic chains and newer cones, and lies on the Trans-Mexican Volcanic Belt, a volcanic arc that runs from coast to coast in central southern Mexico and is formed from the subduction of small tectonic plates beneath the larger North American plate.

BELOW:

Tacaná, Sierra Madre de Chiapas, Mexico/Guatemala
At 4060m (13,320ft), Tacaná (background) is a stratovolcano and the second highest peak in Central America. Despite not having erupted since 1986, and then only mildly, it still threatens the population of a quarter of a million people living nearby. Tacaná is the first volcano on the Central America Volcanic Arc, a 1500km (930 miles) chain of hundreds of volcanic formations that runs parallel to the Pacific coast of Central America and was created by the active subduction zone along the western boundary of the Caribbean plate.

Nevis Peak, Nevis, St Kitts and Nevis, Leeward Islands, Lesser Antilles

Nevis Peak is a 985m (3232ft) stratovolcano with overlapping summit craters located in the centre of the island of Nevis. The mountain has not erupted since prehistory, and its last volcanic activity is unknown. Yet, because of the existence of fumaroles and hot springs at certain places on the slopes, there is still a low level of volcanism, meaning the mountain could one day return to life.

Soufrière Hills, Monsterrat, Leeward Islands, Lesser Antilles
The Soufrière Hills is a complex stratovolcano with a number of lava domes that comprise its summit. It had been dormant for some time when it erupted in 1995, its first eruption in the twentieth century. It has remained active ever since and done untold damage to the small island, leaving more than half of it uninhabitable and causing two-thirds of its 11,500 population to leave.

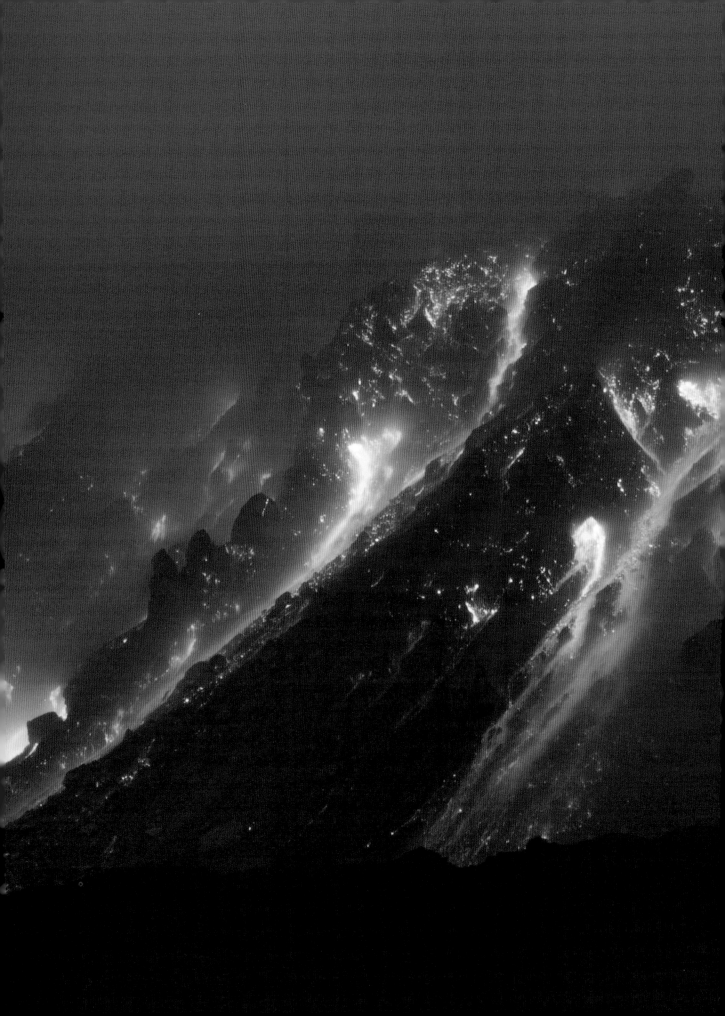

LEFT:

Soufrière Hills, Monsterrat, Leeward Islands, Lesser Antilles
Glowing lava pours from the Soufrière Hills volcano in 2006 after it filled the gap between a growing lava dome in the crater and the crater walls, causing incandescent rockfalls to enter the Tar River Valley. Much of the Caribbean island was coated in 5–7cm (2–3in) of volcanic ash and pebbles.

ABOVE TOP:

Soufrière Hills, Monsterrat, Leeward Islands, Lesser Antilles
The volcanic activity of the Soufrière Hills is characterized by periods of lava dome building and collapse, which cause pyroclastic flows, ash plumes and explosions. One of these explosions led to pyroclastic flows submerging the capital, Plymouth (its courthouse is pictured here), which had already been evacuated, in a deep layer of ash. The island's airport was also destroyed.

ABOVE BOTTOM:

Soufrière Hills, Monsterrat, Leeward Islands, Lesser Antilles
Pyroclastic flows roar down multiple sides of the Soufriere Hills during a 2010 eruption after the collapse of a fountain of tephra. This is just one of many such episodes since the mid-1990s.

Central & South America

The Ring of Fire completes its journey around the Pacific Ocean in the central and southern sections of the American Cordillera, known as the Andes in South America.

Central America lies on the western portion of the Caribbean plate, under which the Cocos plate in the Pacific Ocean, just off the western coast of Central America, is subducted. This forms the Central America Volcanic Arc, and includes the volcanoes of Guatemala, El Salvador, Nicaragua and Costa Rica.

The Andes of South America were created by the subduction of the Nazca and Antarctic plates under the South American plate and are split into four volcanic zones, together known as the Andean Volcanic Belt: the Northern, Central, Southern and Austral. The Northern Volcanic Zone extends from Colombia to Ecuador; the Central Volcanic Zone runs from Peru to Chile (also crossing into Bolivia and Argentina) and forms the western boundary of the Altiplano (Andean Plateau); the South Volcanic Zone extends from roughly the latitude of Santiago, Chile, to Cerro Arenales in Aysén Region; and the Austral Volcanic Zone extends south of the Patagonian Volcanic Gap to the Tierra del Fuego archipelago and is formed from the subduction of the Antarctic plate under the South American plate.

OPPOSITE:

Fuego, Antigua, Guatemala

Fuego has erupted more than 60 times since 1524, making it Central America's most historically active volcano. It is just 16km (9.9 miles) from Guatemala's former capital, Antigua, and is one of three stratovolcanoes overlooking the city. Part of an older volcano, Meseta, lies between 3763m (12,346ft) high Fuego and its twin, Acatenango. Collapse of the ancestral Meseta volcano about 8500 years ago began the growth of the modern Fuego, as they are linked to the same conduit of magma.

LEFT:

Fuego, Antigua, Guatemala
Typically, eruptions of Fuego were of a Vulcanian nature (small yet violent explosions with dense clouds of ash-laden gas and rock, with both pyroclastic and thick magma flows) and lasted a few hours to several days. From 2002, Fuego began a period of almost constant activity that saw bursts of ash and lava, which culminated in an unexpected eruption in 2018 that buried several villages and killed nearly 200 people.

ABOVE:

San Pedro, Guatemala
Lightning flashes over San Pedro volcano, which lies on the western shore of Lake Atitlán and above the village of San Pedro La Laguna. San Pedro is 3020m (9908ft) high and the oldest of three stratovolcanoes constructed within the roughly 85,000-year-old Atitlán III caldera. The date of San Pedro's most recent activity is not known but because it does not display any fumarolic activity it is probably now extinct.

Izalco, El Salvador
Izalco sits on a slope of
Santa Ana volcano. Its black
symmetrical cone formed
from 1770 and the next
200 years saw more than 50
mostly Strombolian eruptions.
During the nineteenth century,
sailors set their course by the
continuous glow from Izalco's
summit, nicknaming it the
'Lighthouse of the Pacific'.

Tiger Island, Gulf of Fonseca, Honduras
Tiger Island is an exctinct basaltic stratovolcano, the peak of which emerges from the sea to form the island. It has a near-symmetrical conical shape and is the southernmost volcano in Honduras. Because of its volcanic past the island's beaches have black sand.

LEFT MIDDLE:
Momotombo, Nicaragua
Momotombo is a stratovolcano, the perfect aesthetic form of which has been popular on designs in Nicaragua for years. Due to the seismic activity and the damage caused to infrastructure during an eruption in 1610, the settlers decided to abandon their city of León (now León Viejo) and relocate to León's present site, 30km (20 miles) to the west.

LEFT BOTTOM:
Concepción, Ometepe Island, Nicaragua
Concepción is the larger of two volcanoes that make up the island of Ometepe, situated in Lake Nicaragua. Because no other volcano has influenced Concepción's formation, it is considered 'pristine'. The volcano sits on weak crust that facilitates magma flow, which increases Concepción's mass and its distortion of the crust. This creates a cyclical pattern of more magma flow and more volcano growth.

OPPOSITE:
El Boquerón, El Salvador
El Boquerón is the main edifice of the San Salvador Volcano, which takes its name from the city over which it looms, and was formed in an old caldera. Its 500m (1640ft) deep crater was made 800 years ago. A 1917 eruption evaporated the lake inside the crater and left behind a small cinder cone named Boqueróncito (pictured).

197

Irazú, Irazú Volcano National Park, Costa Rica
The lagoon of Irazú's circular, steep-walled main crater, one of the volcano's five craters. Irazú is a complex stratovolcano, one of the four volcanoes in Costa Rica's Cordillera Central, and has undergone at least 23 mostly mildly explosive eruptions in historic times. At least two types of lava have been found from different eruptions, suggesting Irazú is fed by two separate magma chambers.

ABOVE:

Irazú, Irazú Volcano National Park, Costa Rica

A peek inside two of Irazú's craters, the main crater and the Diego de la Haya crater, with Turrialba volcano in the background. It is possible to see both the Pacific Ocean and the Caribbean Sea from the summit of either volcano on a clear day, although both are usually shrouded in cloud.

RIGHT:

Turrialba, Turrialba Volcano National Park, Costa Rica

Turrialba has been explosively eruptive in recent years, with ash clouds, ash fall and the presence of toxic gases and acid rain causing the closure of the national park in which it is located, as well as the evacuation of nearby villages. Volcanic material was at times deposited as much as 40km (25 miles) away and reduced visibility for aircraft to the extent that airports across the region were closed.

Arenal, Alajuela, Costa Rica
Dormant for centuries, in 1968 Arenal suddenly returned to life in explosive fashion, birthing three flank craters and burying 15 square km (5.8 sq mi) under rocks, lava and ash, including three small towns. Varying levels of activity continued over the next few decades, such as in January 2009 (pictured), when Arenal underwent sporadic Strombolian eruptions, emitting clouds of gas and flows of lava, which in turn caused occasional avalanches.

Galeras, Colombia
Galeras is a stratovolcano in
the Andes mountain range, and
has erupted numerous times in
the last 500 years. It is the most
active in Colombia and was
designated a Decade Volcano in
1991 because if its proximity to
the 400,000 people of nearby
Pasto. During a 1993 Decade
Volcano conference, a group of
attending scientists mounted an
impromptu expedition to the
crater to to take gas samples
and measurements in order
to be able to predict future
eruptions. An unexpected
eruption while they were
working killed nine people,
including six of the scientists.

OPPOSITE:

Antisana, Quito, Ecuador

Fifty km (31 miles) from Quito is the Andean stratovolcano
Antisana, 5704m (18,714ft) high. An older volcano, now eroded
by glaciers, covers two thirds of the Antisana complex and has two
calderas from earlier explosions. The newer cone emerges on the
northwest side and covers the remaining third.

ABOVE:

Tungurahua, Tungurahua province, Ecuador

Part of the Andean Cordillera Real, along with Antisana,
Tungurahua was built inside an older caldera, which collapsed about
3000 years ago. The volcano has been very active since 1999, with
weeks of Strombolian eruptions at a time, producing ash plumes,
lava and pyroclastic flows, such as here in 2011.

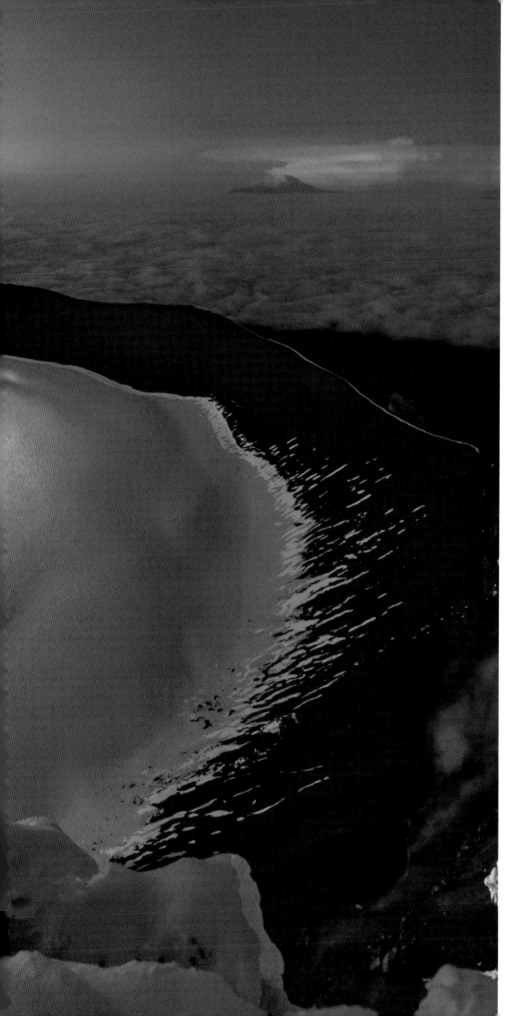

Cotopaxi, Cotopaxi province, Ecuador
A view of Cotopaxi's 800 × 550m (2620 × 1800ft) wide and 250m (820ft) deep crater. It comprises two concentric crater rims, with the outer one being partly free of snow. Cotopaxi is slightly to the southwest of Antisana and is Ecuador's second highest peak at 5897m (19,347ft), and has one of the world's few equitorial glaciers. The volcano has erupted on 85 known occasions and is one of the country's most active volcanoes.

ABOVE TOP:

Cotopaxi, Cotopaxi province, Ecuador

Cotopaxi's biggest known eruptions were in 1742, 1744, 1768 and 1877. The latter three events destroyed Latacunga town on each occasion. During the 1877 eruption, pyroclastic flows on all sides of the mountain melted the entire ice cap to cause lahars that travelled more than 100km (62 miles) to the Pacific Ocean. Modern eruptions threaten flash-melts of the new glacier and lahars that pose a great risk to the land and population nearby.

ABOVE BOTTOM:

Misti, Arequipa, Peru

Misti is a stratovolcano 16km (10 miles) from the city of Arequipa. Inside the summit caldera is a younger crater that itself hosts a yet newer cone with its own crater, making a pattern of three concentric craters. Six Inca mummies and other artifacts were found during excavations near the inner crater in 1998. Misti's proximity to Arequipa and its explosive past make it one of the most dangerous volcanoes in the world.

RIGHT:

Misti, Arequipa, Peru

The long history of eruptions from Misti and its neighbour volcanoes, Chachani and Pichu Pichu, has made the soil extremely fertile and the surrounding area one of the most agriculturally productive in Peru. Residents of Arequipa have also made use of a local white volcanic rock called sillar to construct a significant number of buildings there, which has resulted in Arequipa being nicknamed 'the white city'.

LEFT:
Central Volcanic Zone, Atacama Desert, Chile
The Central Volcanic Zone of the Andes stretches from Peru to Chile, and covers parts of Bolivia and Argentina. It forms the western edge of the Altiplano, or Andean Plateau, the widest section of the Andes. Here a number of volcanoes can be found, including Lascar (left) and Aguas Calientes (centre), close to the Atacama Desert.

ABOVE:
Licancabur, Atacama Desert, Chile/Bolivia
Licancabur lies on the Chile–Bolivia border 40km (25 miles) from the town of San Pedro de Atacama in the Atacama Desert. It has a 400m (1300ft) wide summit crater with a shallow crater lake inside, one of the highest lakes in the world.

OVERLEAF:
Descabezado Grande, Maule Region, Chile
While visually stunning, no volcanic activity has been recorded coming from Descabezado Grande's 1.4km (0.87 miles) wide, ice-filled main crater, and so the volcano is considered dormant. A smaller crater on its northeast side, however, was responsible for an eruption in 1932 and shows ongoing fumarolic activity.

ABOVE:
**Descabezado Grande,
Maule Region, Chile**
These unusual ice formations
decorate the inside of
Descabezado Grande's crater.

RIGHT:
**Central Volcanic
Zone, Chile**
One of the four volcanic zones of
the Andes, the Central Volcanic
Zone has formed because of the
subduction of the Nazca plate
under the South American plate
along the Peru–Chile Trench. The
fissures in the crust this activity
creates allow magma to find
paths to the surface. The lack
of volcanism either side of the
Central Volcanic Zone is thought
to be because of two ridges in
the Nazca plate that enter the
subduction zone at too shallow
an angle to cause any volcanic
activity.

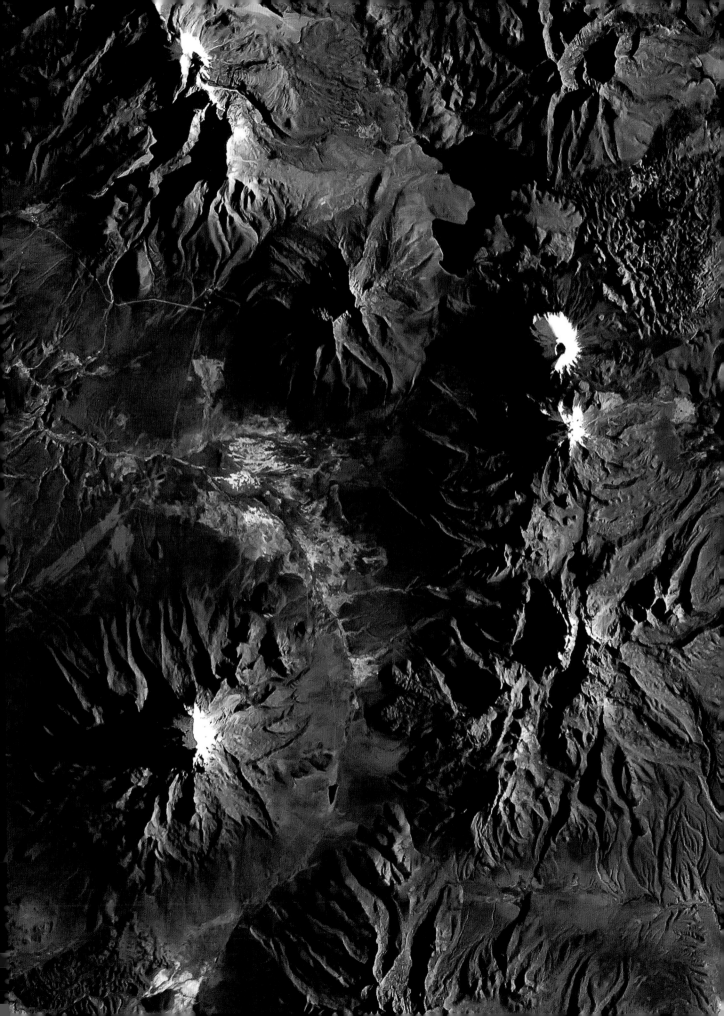

RIGHT:

Juriques and Licancabur,
Atacama Desert, Chile/Bolivia
Juriques (centre) is a parasitic
cone of the larger Licancabur
(left). Its summit reaches an
altitude of 5704m (18,714ft),
208m (682ft) below Licancabur.
The exact age of the last activity
at these two volcanoes is not
known, but lava flows from
the summit and flank vents can
still be detected. At the base of
Juriques, on the Bolivian side
of the border, lies the beautiful
Laguna Verde salt lake, the
striking turquoise colour of
which is caused by arsenic and
other minerals.

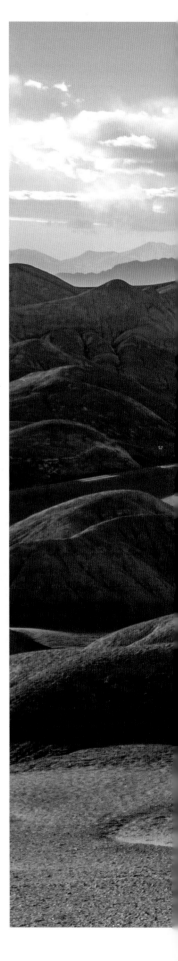

ABOVE:

**Puyehue-Cordón Caulle,
Ranco province, Chile**

Puyehue-Cordón Caulle in the
Southern Volcanic Zone is a
complex of two volcanoes:
Puyehue and the fissure system
of Cordón Caulle. After 51
years of inactivity, in 2011–12
it exploded in what became the
biggest eruption of the twenty-
first century so far. An estimated
100 million tons (102 million
tonnes) of ash, sand and pumice
were ejected, some of which
circled the globe, reaching other
parts of South America, South
Africa, Papua New Guinea,
Australia and New Zealand.

RIGHT:

**Aracar, Salta province,
Argentina**

Aracar, rising in the background
over lava fields, is a conical
stratovolcano just east of the
Chilean border in northwest
Argentina. It formed in three
eruptive phases and sits on
older lava domes. It is arguable
whether it is still active, as no
recent evidence of volcanism
from its 1.5km (0.9 miles) wide
crater – which occasionally fills
with a lake from snowmelt – or
flanks has been seen.

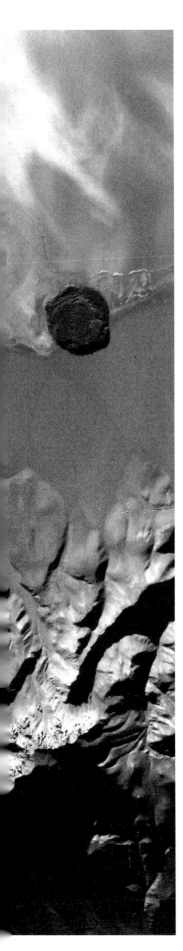

LEFT:

Aracar, Salta province, Argentina
An aerial view of the Andes, with Aracar's lighter-coloured cone centre-left. Nearby, the white dusting of salt coats the land, with the Salar de Arizaro at the upper right. Possibly due to its remoteness, very little is known of Aracar's exact age and history, although it could have been formed by ancient volcanism 266 million years ago. Well-preserved lava flows are found at its base but not higher up its slopes, which would indicate more recent activity.

ABOVE:

Tromen, Neuquén province, Argentina
Tromen is the main structure in a 70km (43 miles) volcanic field, about 150km (93 miles) east of the main volcanic chain that marks the border between Argentina and Chile. Its summit is cut by two overlapping 3.5km (2.1 miles) wide calderas. Historical eruptions of Tromen were reported in the mid-eighteenth century and in 1822.

Picture Credits